MW00990344

UnCoMMon
SENSE

WITHDRAWN

ERAU PRESCOTT LIBRARY

WITHDRAWN

PETER COCHRANE

UNCOMMON SENSE

OUT OF THE BOX THINKING FOR AN IN THE BOX WORLD

Based on the popular silicon.com column

CAPSTONE

11/2007

Copyright © Peter Cochrane 2004

The right of Peter Cochrane to be identified as the authors of this book has been asserted in accordance with the Copyright, Designs and Patents Act 1988

First published 2004 by
Capstone Publishing Limited (A Wiley Company)
The Atrium
Southern Gate
Chichester
West Sussex PO19 8SQ
http://www.wileyeurope.com

All Rights Reserved. Except for the quotation of small passages for the purposes of criticism and review, no part of this publication may be reproduced, stored in a retrieval system or transmitted in any form or by any means, electronic, mechanical, photocopying, recording, scanning or otherwise, except under the terms of the Copyright, Designs and Patents Act 1988 or under the terms of a licence issued by the Copyright Licensing Agency Ltd, 90 Tottenham Court Road, London W1T 4LP, UK, without the permission in writing of the Publisher. Requests to the Publisher should be addressed to the Permissions Department, John Wiley & Sons Ltd, The Atrium, Southern Gate, Chichester, West Sussex PO19 8SQ, England, or emailed to permreq@wiley.co.uk, or faxed to (+44) 1243 770571.

CIP catalogue records for this book are available from the British Library and the US Library of Congress

ISBN 1-84112-477-X

Typeset in Minion 11/16pt by Sparks Computer Solutions Ltd
http://www.sparks.co.uk

Printed and bound by TJ International Ltd, Padstow, Cornwall

10 9 8 7 6 5 4 3 2 1

Substantial discounts on bulk quantities of Capstone Books are available to corporations, professional associations and other organizations.
For details telephone John Wiley & Sons on (+44-1243-770441), fax (+44-1243-770571) or e-mail CorporateDevelopment@wiley.co.uk

Every effort has been made to trace the copyright holders, but if any have been inadvertently overlooked the publishers will be pleased to make the necessary arrangement at the first opportunity.

For Brenda, the bravest girl I ever knew …

Contents

The significant problems we face cannot be solved at the same level of thinking we were at when we created them.

Albert Einstein

Standby

This is a book that expresses the unique view of Peter Cochrane who has watched, and been intimately engaged in, the technology roll-out over the landscape of society for decades. As an observer and commentator he has a great deal to say about the good, the bad and the ugly of the ever-increasing waves of technology deployment. Peter is anything but shy. He is refreshingly frank and honest, surprisingly accessible, and so is this book. It is a no-holds-barred presentation that will entertain, explain and challenge the layperson and the expert.

Basically, this is a collection of essays from Peter that strips away the hype and mystery surrounding 'conventional wisdom', and exposes the realities and truths in the sense of 'the emperor's new clothes'. He sees, reaches, and extracts the essence of an issue, and presents the results in a clear and passionate fashion. Peter forces the reader to see, think, and re-evaluate many long-held opinions in a fresh and logical fashion.

Uncommon Sense is, in Peter's words, '… a book about living, rather than just surviving in a world of more technology and more change that our species has experienced hitherto.' He expresses his thoughts in dramatic terms, making ample use of graphics and images to drive home his point; in many ways, the book is defined by his use of graphics and symbology. His goal is to set straight the confused thinking that surrounds much of the technology to which the end user has been subject. Peter has little patience for poor presentation of ideas and bemoans the ineptitude of most scientific presentations. He elaborates on the weakness of many of today's management approaches, as well as on the failure of many technologies themselves.

He points out that it is often a lack of imagination that limits the impact and effect of the information technology revolution. He properly recognizes that wireless communications and access will be omnipresent, and addresses some of the impediments that have been thrown up that have slowed down the deployment of a full wireless infrastructure.

Peter further points out the non-intuitive behaviour of exponential growth and how it has fooled so many bright people who fail to recognize its impact. He addresses the enormous complexity that is part of the technological and societal revolution by illustrating the true meaning of exponential growth, chaotic action, and counterintuitive outcomes.

One of Peter's pet peeves and frustrations is technology that fails to deliver what was promised. He is also irritated by managers who don't understand that they don't understand, and politicians who take a disastrously focused (single or limited issue) view in order to survive rather than improve things. His dialogue and illustrations take us through the causes of technology failure and the unlikeliness of it truly recovering. For example he cites and comments on hospital records, broadband, 3G, eShopping, the local loop and last mile as continuing to present nasty and, as yet, unsolved problems of effective deployment and delivery. Peter's holistic views address issues that span the important and vital through to the apparently trivial – for example the availability of pornography on the net, the futility of personal filing systems on a PC, and control freak managers.

From a more global point of view, Peter makes the case that if we are to make any progress in solving the world's critical problems, we must apply our advanced computer modelling capability to quantify the interaction between the variables, and predict the impact of these variables on the outcomes. He argues that the problems and their interactions are far too complex for the unaided human intellect to cope with, and this applies to the various summits that continue to meet, discuss, and fail to bring light to these issues.

Peter recognizes that the world we are moving to in this 21st century is one of embedded technology, intelligent agents, mobile access, and vast, fast networks. In this world, he sees a need for clarity and vision. It can be a magnificent place to live in, but it will not be without addressing the serious issues of privacy, security, intellectual property challenges and ethical issues.

In this book you will be entertained, amazed, concerned, challenged and invigorated by the bright future that technology is offering. It will take uncommon sense and fresh thinking to truly tame this future and make the most of it. Enjoy!

Leonard Kleinrock, UCLA, November 2003

Where Did This Book Come From?

Genesis

For me 1995 was the year when the great IT and dot-com frenzy started, and 2001 was the year it all came to a crashing halt. It was an exciting time for sure, and we made great progress on all fronts, but eventually the energy expired and the dot-com crash arrived. I had been in the thick of it, developing new technologies and writing of the likely consequences in a weekly column for the *Daily Telegraph*. I had also contributed to the *Guardian*, *The Times*, *Australian*, *USA Today*, *New York Times* and *Sentaku* et al.

Collapse

In just six short months most of the technology columns closed down, but I kept writing and publishing on www.cochrane.org.uk which resulted in a continued correspondence with an established and energetic global readership – people were still clearly interested even if the media were not!

Focus

So it was that in May 2002 Tony Hallett called and asked me to write a new weekly column for the www.silicon.com news and information service. This I agreed to do and got underway with an 850-word column that encouraged readers to comment, debate and email. The popularity of the column fostered a further relationship with Mark Allin of Wiley-Capstone Books. And so the plot was hatched to turn the columns into a book.

Mission

My purpose in writing and broadcasting had always been to explain and alert people to future challenges and current changes invoked by technology, or a lack of it! And my emphasis was always on a clear and concise, 'make-em-think', format that looked for the novel and the explicit. Hence, in content and style this book is purposely different – and associated with my home page www.cochrane.org.uk.

Thanks

- The silicon.com readership not only acted as observers, but online commentators and editors with their numerous and varied inputs subsumed into this expanded and illuminated text.
- Tony Hallett (my silicon.com editor), John Moseley and Mark Allin (my Wiley-Capstone editors) were responsible for numerous inputs, suggestions and guidance that enriched the final product.
- Michaela Cozens considerably augmented my efforts by doing a lot of the typing, pre-printing, collation and general support at all kinds of strange hours as I traversed the planet – emailing when and where I could.
- My daughter Sarah did a super job of editing and researching, as well as keeping me on the straight and narrow. She is also responsible for whatever order you might detect in the final presentation.
- John Duggan at Sparks, and the graphics, editorial and production folks at Wiley-Capstone turned out to be a dream to work with and gave me lots of support and help.
- My colleagues, friends, family, general public, politicians, managers, companies and organizations are all featured in this book somewhere, but they will never figure out where or how!

To all of you I owe a debt of gratitude in helping me bring to fruition a different view and presentation ... I just hope I have done justice to the human condition, our technologies, and our past, present and future.

Peter Cochrane, Martlesham Heath, UK, February 2004

Byte oo
Boot Up

When I was a young child at school and first started to read, there was an ever-present pressure for me to move on from one book to another, away from pictures and towards a world exclusively dedicated to words. But I fell in love with images at an early age and still remember with some affection the magic of Rupert Bear, and excitement of Dan Dare, Superman, Batman and more. The education process was relentless, and soon I was lost in a world of words and no pictures, where my imagination conjured up new visions to go with Robinson Crusoe, The Three Musketeers and Horn Blower et al. Just once a week there was a ritual visit to the movies to see Errol Flynn, John Wayne and other hero's paint their vivid pictures across the silver screen. For me this was a wonderful escape from the reality of an austere post-WWII UK and black and white print.

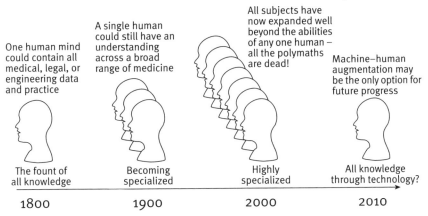

No one knows anything any more...
...teams are vital – not an option

One human mind could contain all medical, legal, or engineering data and practice

A single human could still have an understanding across a broad range of medicine

All subjects have now expanded well beyond the abilities of any one human – all the polymaths are dead!

Machine–human augmentation may be the only option for future progress

The fount of all knowledge | Becoming specialized | Highly specialized | All knowledge through technology?

1800 | 1900 | 2000 | 2010

If only it was all this simple...

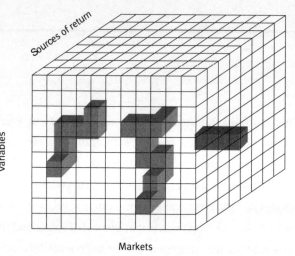

Almost nothing we deal with is confined to just three dimensions

We are mostly faced with so many that we have to simplify the picture and take an aggregate decision on the biggest parameters

In a complex non-linear world simplification can be very dangerous!

Industry dimensions

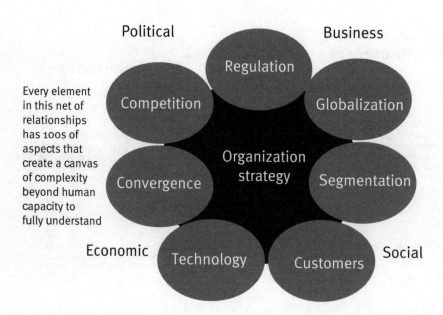

Every element in this net of relationships has 100s of aspects that create a canvas of complexity beyond human capacity to fully understand

Political

Business

Regulation

Competition

Globalization

Organization strategy

Convergence

Segmentation

Economic

Technology

Customers

Social

Throughout my education and, later, professional life I returned to pictures as I became increasingly dependent on graphics to aid and abet my basic understanding. I gradually became aware that my slow and laboured progress in mathematics and science was almost entirely down to the limited artistry and lack of clarity and thinking of my early teachers. I systematically failed one class after another and gained almost nothing of worth from my schooling spanning the years 5–15, barring a mechanistic way of solving set problems with known answers.

Much later in my teens I encountered teachers, lecturers and professors with an ability to get down to my ignorance level, able to see my difficulty, and find analogies and pictures (on paper and in the mind) that allowed me to see and understand with greater clarity and insight. Even in the most esoteric of mathematical, scientific, engineering and technological corners, I still rely heavily on pictures. In fact, I consider mathematics to be both a language and a very powerful visualization tool. Unfortunately, this is a tool denied to 99.9% of all peoples due to the universally poor standards of teaching and understanding of the topic.

Now, at the age of 57, I have, in some respects, begun to resent words, resent the time spent reading and writing. To me there has to be a better way. If you permit me, an adaptation of an old adage:

If a picture is worth 1000 words,
a moving picture is worth 1,000,000 words, and
an animated multimedia experience is worth 1,000,000,000 words.

Why do people write so much and say so little; why don't they say what they mean and mean what they say? It is as if brevity and honesty have gone out of fashion. When we communicate we should remember that face-to-face is not video-conferencing, or a telephone call, a radio or TV interview, and further, a letter is not a fax, email, or text message. Moreover, none of these are the printed page or multimedia – but people still try to compare and say that one is better than the other. Such arguments are futile, each has pros and cons, and each has a very useful and appropriate place. Today we have more ways of communicating effectively and efficiently than ever before, but the key problem is that people confuse and misuse them.

So why am I writing another book? I still give many lectures and presentations a year, and my Web site still receives over 1000 visits per week, and I find much confusion and doubt on critical issues and topics we all need to understand. I also find much flawed and confused thinking, not to mention misinformation and unwise policies used and enacted. When Capstone approached me, I made it clear that I had no interest in writing a conventional book. In my view, a book about living in a fast-moving, IT-dominated world with no pictures, animation and interaction, would see most of what I wish to communicate lost in a sea of inadequate words. It would be like a philosopher or theologian explaining the meaning of life – a complete waste of time. So, from the outset it was agreed that I could include more pictures than words and relate the whole to my active and growing Web site – www.cochrane.org.uk.

Buying this book gives you more than a passport to my thoughts, words and pictures, you get access to everything I can contribute with all the media we have to hand in 2003. My concern is to try to communicate the complex and inaccessible in a clear and concise way. My primary fear is that the orthogonal nature of clarity and truth may defeat both reader and author.

We seek clarity and truth...
...but they are mostly orthogonal...

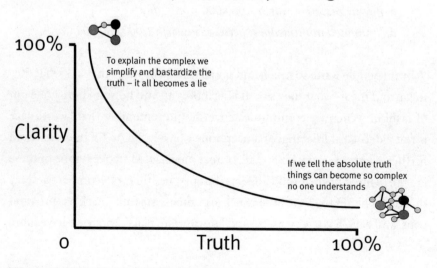

100%

To explain the complex we simplify and bastardize the truth – it all becomes a lie

Clarity

If we tell the absolute truth things can become so complex no one understands

0   Truth   100%

Axiom 1: Mutually exclusive...

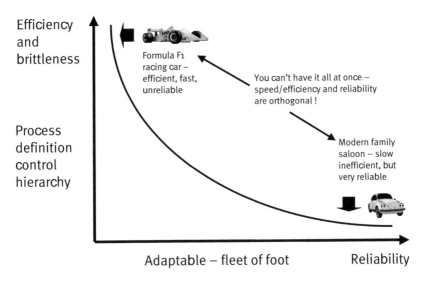

Efficiency and brittleness

Process definition control hierarchy

Formula F1 racing car – efficient, fast, unreliable

You can't have it all at once – speed/efficiency and reliability are orthogonal !

Modern family saloon – slow inefficient, but very reliable

Adaptable – fleet of foot   Reliability

Axiom 2: Mutually exclusive...

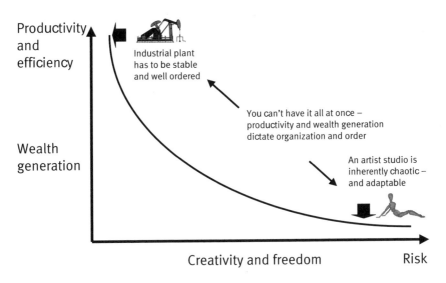

Productivity and efficiency

Wealth generation

Industrial plant has to be stable and well ordered

You can't have it all at once – productivity and wealth generation dictate organization and order

An artist studio is inherently chaotic – and adaptable

Creativity and freedom   Risk

As a general rule, reducing descriptions and explanations to the simplest level so we can communicate quickly and others can understand sufficiently, insults the depth of the problem and blankets the audience in blissful ignorance. We always ride a curve of absolute truth to the blatant lie, and absolute clarity to total confusion. My mission is to neither insult nor confuse, but to communicate and explain with as much clarity as I can muster.

As the Chinese say, we live in interesting times. We now see the simple (and linear) being overtaken by unbridled complexity, when order is negated by chaos, when technology is pushing us individually and as organizations faster than we can adapt and adopt. I have lived on the cusp of the new for the past 30 years, and have experimented with future technologies and systems that have yet to appear, and this book is my attempt at explaining some of what has happened, what is happening and what is about to happen – it is about readying for the future and changing the way we think.

There is no set order to the text or indeed the pictures, although the illustrations and pictures do relate to the associated page set. My home page contains even more data and illustrations and is the repository of almost all that I ever did or thought - www.cochrane.org.uk. So you can dip into the text and pictures at any point, see what takes your eye and interest, and explore. It is all designed to make you think, question and, I hope, understand more of this new age in which we live. But even more importantly – enjoy. This is a book about living, rather than just surviving in a world of more technology and more change that our species has experienced hitherto. It is also a book written by someone who has struggled every day to understand everything he encountered since he was truly cognitive. Someone who didn't easily fit into a rigid and unthinking education, system and corporate world, and someone who believes in investing time and effort, trying, testing and contributing – no matter what.

In compiling this book I have attempted to meet the needs of the amateur and professional, to make the expert and the lay think, to promote the right debate, and promote right questions. We are all challenged by change, and we all have to find our own survival strategy, and it need not be full of stress and worry, it can be full of fun. Discovery, understanding and realization are fun!

Peter Cochrane

At my home on a not so warm UK spring evening, wearing a thick shirt with the sleeves rolled down, drinking great coffee, in a garden full of new life, colour and scent, watching the sun go down – with my Apple G4 laptop linked to the www via a WiFi (802.11 link).

Martlesham Heath,
Suffolk, UK

Byte 01
Education That Doesn't Fit

We were all fed a diet of problems with solutions from our earliest days until we graduated. Teachers and professors had no choice but to prescribe problems that had a clear definition and route to solution.

Almost all the mathematics, science and technology in our schools come from a prescriptive box. Students expect a clearly defined problem, a logical analysis, and clear solution. What's more, so do the academic staff and the education system. This creates mindsets that think our universe is full of problems with solutions, and that there is only a small proportion of problems that we are still trying to solve. You don't have to be out of school and into industry for very long to realize our universe is not a well-behaved place and, in fact, the converse is true.

By looking at the night sky and observing clusters of constellations, or watching the cataclysmic events on our own planet, we can quickly see that chaos is actually the natural mode rather than the exception. Natural disasters come in clusters, as do births, deaths, marriages, car accidents, and electrical appliance failures in our homes. There is also ample evidence to suggest that Mother Nature's natural mode is also chaotic. The boom/bust cycles in economies that politicians seek to smooth are also symptomatic of non-linear mechanisms. Some of the chaotic mechanisms are easy to understand, but many are not. The reality is that we have very little appreciation of the true magnitude and impact of non-linear systems.

Throughout my education I had a vision of a universe that was enclosed and well behaved, with some remote and small region that we didn't understand, which we avoided at all costs. My earliest industrial periods quickly corrected that view as most of the problems and the solutions that

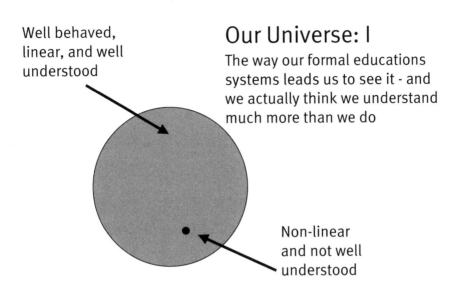

Well behaved, linear, and well understood

Our Universe: I
The way our formal educations systems leads us to see it - and we actually think we understand much more than we do

Non-linear and not well understood

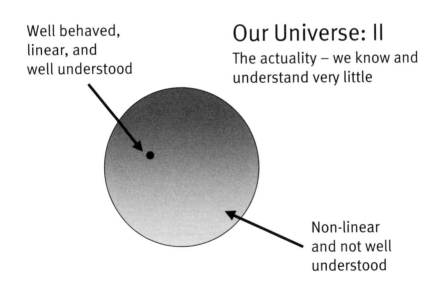

Well behaved, linear, and well understood

Our Universe: II
The actuality – we know and understand very little

Non-linear and not well understood

had been put in front of me were mostly approximations and distortions of the truth.

For the millennia we got away with applying linear thinking and limited models to complex non-linear situations and derived adequate answers. Everything you use today, from telephone, television, mobile phone to automobile, has been created using material, systems, scientific and mathematical models that have been adequate from an engineering perspective. They were good enough to get the job done.

It has always seemed paradoxical that ancient man, making fire, stumbled on the bow and arrow and the ability to create a very rapid rotation of a pointed stick using the bow to convert lateral to rotary motion. To make the giant leap to the watchmakers lathe and the integrated circuit is astounding, but once we had hit on the idea that rotary motion allowed great precision, we could progress from the honing of saplings to create accurate dowels for arrows, to create the wooden lathe, followed by the metal lathe and today's precision manipulators.

This says you can take something very crude and continually refine it to create something extremely precise. This is exactly what has been happening across the broad front of our progress. Our mathematics, science, engineering and technology have all stood on the shoulders of previous

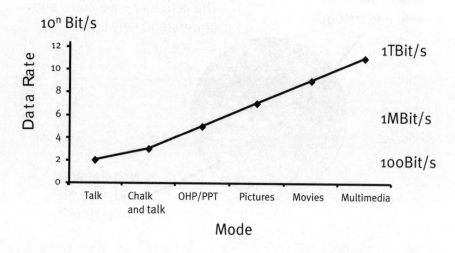

Education modes and bits...

10^n Bit/s

Data Rate — Mode

Influence and degrees of separation...
and distance to information and expertise

		Separation						
		1	2	3	4	5	6	7
Number of people you know or can email	10	10^2	10^3	10^4	10^5	10^6	10^7	10^8
	10^2	10^4	10^6	10^8	10^{10}			
	10^3	10^6	10^9					
	10^4	10^8						

Population an individual can influence or reasonably expect to access for help

generations to give us greater understanding, knowledge, capability and complexity. Refinement is not confined to physical artefacts that we manufacture, it also applies to models, ideas and systems; it is a universal polish that goes hand in hand with progress.

Many of the chaos-generating mechanisms are surprising. My favourite is coffee, which brings down telecommunications networks every day. The mechanism is delightful. Take for example 1000 people listening to the morning speaker at a conference, with no telephone calls being made or received. At 10:15 coffee arrives and 300 mobile phones are switched on. Within seconds, the network is overloaded and crashes.

Coffee has become a strange attractor, as have freeway accidents, which prompt localized telephone calls to bring down the mobile telephone network. Delayed flights, trains and question times on some radio and TV phone-in programmes invoke similarly chaotic responses.

Recent years have seen mighty corporations with illustrious histories brought down in a few months. The apparently insignificant actions of accountants have destroyed complete industries, pension funds and the lives of people who were once proud to work for those companies. How did it all happen and why didn't we see it coming? The reality of business is that

Routes to understanding

- Philosophers = Let's think how a chicken works
- Physicists = Let's dissect a chicken
- Engineers = Let's build a chicken
- *Software engineers = Let's specify a chicken*

for the most part we're now moving at a pace that is faster then most CEOs, boards and managers can digest.

I have always questioned the fact that the military play games all day and occasionally have a war; in industry we are at war every day and we never stop to play. We have no models capable of predicting the outcome of our business actions. We desperately need to start modelling and wargaming to hone our strategic thinking. A once-in-three-years away day is not enough! If we do not create new tools we will see the business casualty rate increase.

Those in charge of industry who continue with their linear thinking and limited perspective will continue making wrong decisions. This is both dangerous and increasingly serious. Building a facsimile of a company, with a government, regulator and competition, to play an n-dimensional game of chess is the basic element missing. Here, thousands of moves can be tried and the outcomes examined.

Computer simulations could be created, where we input new starting conditions and run computer models time and time again to see what the range of outcomes will be. In industry we see people taking the most obvious parameters to perform a superficial analysis to then make bad decisions. This is demonstrably flawed. They have to become more sophisticated or die!

Byte 02
Conference Turnaround

Gone are the days when audiences would hold their breath in anticipation of nothing getting from computer to projector.

I'm in the USA at a conference with 100 people from organizations based all over the planet. Every seat has a power outlet, a high-speed LAN connection, microphone for questions, voting button, and a WiFi access. I can see 62 laptops scattered around the room and 59 screens are up and running. There are also a large number of PDAs and a minority using paper. As I walk around the room at least 20 are doing their email, about 10 are writing documents, a couple are doing complex graphics, and the rest seem to be searching the Web.

The first speaker is using all the latest PC and net technology available and giving an unusual business model overview that seems to have limited appeal. His delivery style is interesting but somewhat monotonic. Only a few people are sticking with it and the majority are busy working on their laptops. Having recently watched the movie *Gladiator*, I have the feeling he is being given a collective 'thumbs down' on content at least. But he soldiers on addressing the interested few!

Europeans are often taken aback by American directness and usually read it as rudeness rather than efficiency. The protocol of the two continents is entirely different! In this experimental environment, the response of the audience has been almost unanimous, and little time has been wasted. In Europe a similar conference would have this speaker wasting 100 man-hours of (audience) life for every hour he was talking. But not here; people are vaguely listening with one ear whilst getting on with productive activities. Very little productive and creative time is being wasted as most are simultaneously connected to several arenas other than this one.

Finally, the speaker reaches the punchline, receives his applause, has few questions from the audience, unplugs and retires – his golden opportunity to influence 100 mindsets has been missed. I wander back to my seat and start typing these words as the next speaker sets up. I relax in the knowledge that I can continue working and thinking irrespective of the quality of the remaining presenters. As it turns out the next presenters in the series are younger and with a higher energy level, have great content augmented by excellent presentation material and, most importantly, have an engaging style and delivery.

To gauge the audience impact I keep going to the back of the room for a coffee to scan the room activity. None of the screens are closed down, but there is less keyboard and mouse activity and it looks as though a larger percentage of imaginations have been captured. Along with the rest of the audience I keep listening and working with an enhanced attention span focused on these new speakers and their material. The availability of the materials online also affords the audience the advantage of being able to annotate and record the content to hard drive in a semi real-time environment.

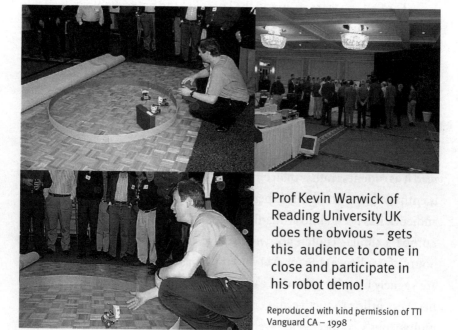

Prof Kevin Warwick of Reading University UK does the obvious – gets this audience to come in close and participate in his robot demo!

Reproduced with kind permission of TTI Vanguard CA – 1998

This conference modus operandi is almost unique and, for me, one of the most productive formats I've experienced, with all the technology used to enhance the experience rather than detract from it. It is always unfortunate and annoying when someone arrives at a conference ill-prepared and ill-equipped. To wander on to the stage with overhead slides resembling the Dead Sea Scrolls, a laptop computer you can't drive, and then fumbling in front of the audience for half an hour getting the right slide set sorted out, is unprofessional and time wasting. It is also highly embarrassing all round.

If you are prepared and the technology goes wrong everyone is sympathetic, but these days that is seldom the case. Gone are the days when people would hold their breath in anticipation of nothing coming from the computer to the projector and screen. I wish more presenters would acknowledge their responsibility to the audience to be well prepared and professional, and to stretch the technology to the limit so that they can communicate in a short time what has probably taken them years to understand.

There are a few more innovations I would like to see. A direct link from projector to my laptop so I could capture all of the pictures and movies direct would be really convenient. Most leading-edge speakers never supply material in advance as they generally prepare right up to the last minute, adjusting their presentation in accord with the prior speakers. If they supply their materials at all it is after the event, but it would be far easier to deposit those bits in real time. It would also be relatively easy to record the spoken word to be included with the presentation materials.

I would also like another facility for the speakers. I think an interest and comprehension indicator based on audience voting or keyboard and mouse activity would be really useful – more especially if it was visible to both the speaker and audience. I've often craved such a facility when presenting over video links. It is very difficult to present to a TV camera or a sheet of glass and, more often that not, the audience audio feedback is considerably subdued in an attempt to limit any acoustic problems. As a presenter in front of an audience you depend upon eye contact and body language as well as the acoustic. I think we could enhance the experience with a few electronic indications when people are in fact engaged and literally online.

People express themselves differently face-to-face, by telephone, email and written letter. In classroom and lecture theatres peer pressure, time and numbers stilt protocols, but an additional indicator set from voting and keyboard could add a new dimension. No more embarrassment at admitting to a lack of understanding, or requesting a slowdown. I think that the anonymity of the eWorld could be a real positive!

Byte 03
Salesmanship

Watching technologists sell their ideas to customers is like an evening at the Moscow State open-air strip club in January watching the dance of the 99 rabbit skins.

It seems to be that PowerPoint is single-handedly responsible for the demise of the human race's ability to tell a story. Every presentation session I seem to attend sees the audience subjected to 'Death by PowerPoint'. This method of presentation has become the dominant mode in all company meetings and conferences everywhere on the planet. And whilst the base technology is incredibly powerful, time and again I see people reading the words that are already on their slides, failing to get to the punchline quickly, and delving into far too much irrelevant detail just because it is possible. They also seem to have lost the ability to adapt and step out of the A–Z sequence, and more often than not, it is about as interesting as watching paint dry! Where is the humour, the candour, originality, sparkle, fun even?

The worst example I can recall of technology misuse, supported by a complete lack of imagination, was demonstrated at a conference on virtual reality. The first three presenters used overhead slides containing only words, without a single picture! What a great opportunity they missed, to inject movies, animations, diagrams, excitement and a physical demonstration of what was being described. It might be that they were rushing to publish and had nothing to show, but without a shadow of a doubt, they imparted more boredom than understanding. Had they never heard of demo or die?

It is always important to communicate effectively and to help others comprehend. It is even more important to get organizations to make the right decisions in the shortest possible time. I often despair at the time

The telephone service in 2000 AD

'The telephone service will reach practically every household and be a real maid of all work. All exchanges will be automatic. Computer techniques will be used to test and maintain the equipment, deal with operating difficulties, settle subscribers' queries and – especially in the international network – decide how calls should be routed.

'There will be direct subscriber calling everywhere. Push button methods, coupled with simplified selective codes for frequently called numbers, electronic switching and digital code signalling will all speed up the service.

'The telephone will incorporate other new features. It could be a picturephone with loudspeaking facilities. Subscribers will be able to dial in to computer libraries and get a playback of any audio or audiovisual tape available, either on their picturephones or on their ordinary television sets.

'Information and news of all kinds will be on tape from computer information centres. Housewives will be able to key into suppliers' installations to do their picture shopping and even pay their bills from home.

'Telecommunications will also relieve the housewife of the need to stay in as well as to go out. Answering facilities will deal with calls and callers: she will be able to run her home from outside by giving instructions either directly to her domestic equipment, or to a household robot; and meters for household services will be read, and the bills rendered and paid over lines.'
– *Read by the Rt. Hon. Edward Short, MP, UK 24 June, 1967*

A prime example of bad presentation material. When projected you can't see it let alone read it!

wasted in discussion and debate predicated by poor briefing, presentations and the sheer inability to adapt to an audience.

It may seem a strange admission for a scientist and engineer, but I secretly admire the producers of TV adverts. A strange choice you might think, but they convince us to purchase things we didn't know we needed, and they get us to part with more money that we would rationally admit to.

Medium and communication

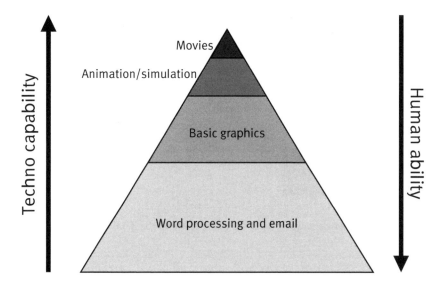

If only more people were able to approach their brevity, focus and efficiency of communication.

Over the years I have watched numerous technologists sell their products and ideas to customers and management. More often that not, it is like an evening at the Moscow State open-air strip club in January. The star comes onto the stage to perform the dance of the 99 rabbit skins, but by the time she gets to the last one, the audience are so cold they don't care any more and just want to go home. Car salesmen don't start with the concept of transport, the invention of the wheel, the detail of the internal combustion engine and traction control. They get the customer in the car and demonstrate the acceleration, the road holding and the hi-fi. In short, they impress the heck out of the customer and if they should ask a question, then they show them the engine compartment and other features.

When was the last time you looked under the hood of a car you were purchasing, or indeed took the back off a TV, or the lid off the top of a washing machine before you decided to buy? Who cares? They are just boxes we purchase by the colour of their buttons and switches. Design, look, feel,

Guess who?

Just 352 pixels – we don't need all of the detail to recognize a face or grasp an idea ...

functionality, quality of service and value is what we crave, and the 'how' is now of little or no direct interest.

It is really astonishing that technologists and engineers seem to be the worst offenders. They have all the technology and opportunity imaginable to present what they have done in an exciting and riveting way. Two of the most cataclysmic examples I have ever witnessed involved a university professor delivering a lecture on multimedia using black and white OHPs, and an engineer using mathematical equations to describe a natural language computer interface that he referred to as the 4D metaphor. How could they get it so wrong? Why didn't they just do a full-frontal demo?

Looking at our education inside and outside of our formal schooling, college and university system, we are all conditioned by years of A–Z serial progressions, linear thinking. Understanding through logical argument, experimentation, demonstration and blind indoctrination, is basically what we have been subjected to. Yet this doesn't sell cars or technology and it doesn't win over an audience who are pressured, preoccupied and in a hurry. We have the technology to produce and present brilliant low-cost graphics, animations and simulations. It is hard to find a better tool for communicating what is in prospect.

The most common excuse is 'I don't have time', or worse, 'I cannot afford the investment in equipment or training to become competent.' I suppose we could apply the same misguided rationale to reading and writing, which most of us invest in throughout our entire lives. I've always thought that there was more than a grain of wisdom in the old Chinese proverb:

'I hear and I forget, I see and I remember, I do and I understand.'

It is so easy with modern technology to let the customer have hands-on experience, to let them play, try it out, and ask questions. We should allow them to decide their path of understanding. It is presumptuous to dictate how others might think and understand.

In our entire history there has never been a time when technology and opportunity has been so exciting, but it would appear that the opportunity to be boring has also accelerated and been magnified. We all know what is possible and our expectations have been raised by the media and movie industry. It is our individual responsibility to consider our audience, what they know, and what they don't, what they are interested in, and how receptive they might be, and what would excite and interest them. These are the key questions we should be asking.

The Coming Oil Crisis

The biggest challenge for us this year?

It is 1 January 2003 and I am reflecting on the events of the past year and their historical context, trying to formulate a general prognosis. Just what is going to happen? What are the major issues facing humanity? Is there a single dominant issue that will impact on all others? Ruling out some super volcano, massive meteor impact, nuclear or biological war that would wipe us from the surface of the planet, I can see just one key and immediate problem beyond overpopulation – and that is energy.

The predictions for the discovery of new oil reserves (their size, availability and economic viability) indicate global production will peak during the period 2003–05 and then we will see the start of a general and irrevocable decline. Yet energy demand will continue to expand and may even accelerate as the Second World industrializes, and the First World refuses to back off on its assumed luxuries.

The richest nations are unlikely to back off their demand, and may even continue current expansion rates. US oil production peaked in 1970, while EU (insignificant) North Sea production peaked around 2001. But both have the economic muscle to respond to higher prices to the disadvantage of those lower down the league table of prosperity. All the recent evidence is that they will do just that.

For those who think natural gas and 'green' alternatives are going to save the situation, my advice is: don't hold your breath. Supplies of natural gas are in rapid decline too, and the green alternatives are insignificant, mostly impractical, or insufficiently developed to make a real contribution.

Global oil production – aggregated projections

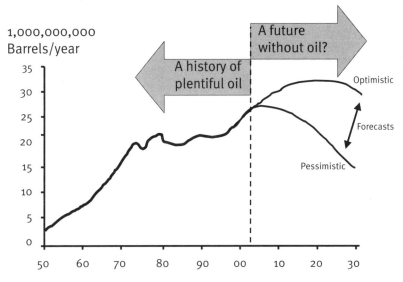

How long do we have before we face a major global crisis on an irreversible scale? About ten years at most!

As far as I can see there is only one developed technology and industrial country in a good position to face such a crisis. France established the largest nuclear power programme to date and is the closest to energy self-sufficiency. Nuclear power stands alone as the only technology available with a proven ability to fill the energy gap. That is not to say that there may not be viable alternatives, just that they are not readily available in production quantities.

The bad news is that it takes a decade to design, build and commission a nuclear power station. While nuclear power output grew around 30% last year, it still only supplies about 16% of the world total. As I write there are 36 new nuclear plants under construction globally, but the planet actually needs hundreds to meet the demand in energy growth, and to displace the huge CO_2 (and C^{14} nuclear) pollution produced by coal- and gas-fired power stations. In the US and the EU, new nuclear plant construction is more or less zero. I am not going to address the political and emotional aspects here as they pose a real, and very irrational, showstopper.

% Oil consumption by sector

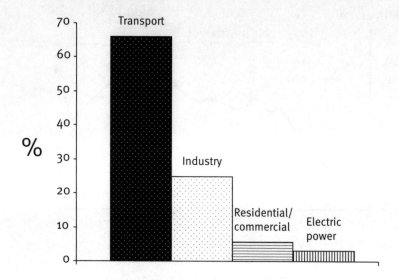

Burning hydrocarbons always seemed to me to be a huge mistake as it may cause climatic change and wastes a resource we need for plastics, pharmaceuticals, building materials, infrastructure components and more. We have to stop burning oil and coal and we have no choice. The crunch is rapidly approaching.

What is going to happen as the oil noose tightens over the next ten years? Without doubt the most immediate and biggest impact will be in the area of physical transport. Goodbye cheap and abundant flights, hello higher petrol/gas prices. Collectively we are all going to travel less in the coming decades unless we can find one or more viable alternatives.

Next will be heat, air-conditioning, light and power. It could become a less comfortable and less bright life seeing us more at the mercy of weather – colder houses and offices in colder climates and hotter in the hotter climes.

Is there going to be any sector that will prosper from the coming energy crisis? Telecoms and IT are the only sectors delivering more for less, year on year, and they are in a position to replace some physical travel.

Beyond what we have already, we can expect to see video conferencing that actually works. There will be the possibility of remote medical monitoring of patients – including drug and medicine administration, plus the teleportation of people and expertise using VR, augmented VR and telepresence technologies. Unlike the energy sector, all of these technologies have been developed, tried and tested, and are on the pre-production shelf ready to go.

Can I see a bright light of opportunity? Yes, but not this morning. It is cloudy and raining. On average about 1kW of energy falls on every square metre of the planet every day from the sun – but we don't collect it. Enough energy falls on the roof of my house to make it self-sufficient for all my family's power needs, only I have no means of economically collecting or storing it. *The material and energy cost of equipping every home with such technology today would see the planet die even faster!*

Mother Nature has given us an existence theorem – photosynthesis, an efficient photonic-to-biological energy converter. So far we have created the chemical and physical models, new materials and computing power to take on this major and most vital problem. But we have not invested heavily in this direction.

I can see a host of less significant problems looming in the coming decades but the technologies are waiting to be discovered and solutions to be created. We have all the basic tools. All we need is the political and financial will. Since 9/11 the investment in fundamentally new technology has been near zero. When the money tap is turned back on, we need to address our future energy needs in order to maintain our progress and avert other crisis situations. From where I am standing, 2003 and beyond looks like being a fun ride.

Byte 05
Summits, Models and Machines

Some of the biggest problems facing humanity – and there are quite
a few – are crying out for solutions based on computer modelling.

This past summer it was difficult to miss the gathering of world leaders at
the Johannesburg summit. I remember watching a TV debate of 20 or so
well-educated delegates drawn from different countries and creeds. There
was also a studio audience making comments and contributions. Everyone
seemed intelligent, thoughtful and sincere.

The TV presenter introduced guests and audience members, and
posed the serious question of the evening: *'What are the two key problems*
facing humanity?'

The first delegate who was asked suggested clean water and AIDS,
the second energy and poverty, the third refugees and climatic change, the
fourth pollution and rainforest destruction. So it went on: terrorism, arms
control, ozone depletion, nuclear weapons, arms sales, gun control, drugs,
globalization, and many more. At no point was there any direct agreement.

The programme moved on swiftly, but there was never any focus, only
heated views: 'It is all the fault of the multinationals'; 'Nuclear power and
GM crops must be banned'; 'Alternative medicine is best'; 'The planet can
look after itself'.

You could name any extremist group and they all seemed to be there.
The entire programme ultimately came to an indeterminate and useless
end. It seemed to be a microcosm of the summit – a lot of hot air, but no
change! What chance is there that thousands of delegates, from hundreds
of countries, would find any correlation of opinion? None! What are they
doing sitting there with their piles of paper, each fighting their corner for

Estimated adult/child deaths from HIV/AIDS – 2002 (millions)

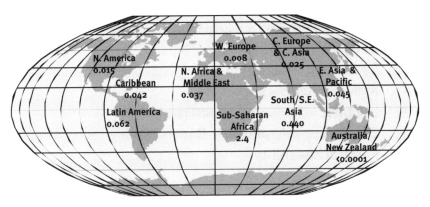

Source: World Health Organization

their individual interests and beliefs? Where are the machines? Where are the models? Where is the raw data, the study reports? Where is a process that would allow them to see what is actually key?

The truth is, none of us have a clue what the key threat to humanity really is. We are fundamentally incapable of identifying and solving such problems until it is too late, as we are limited by thought and imagination in an n-dimensional space where n >> 3. Without the assistance of computer models that relate data and decisions to actual outcomes, we are going to be lost in a sea of meaningless heated debate. Acting on perceived threats almost always means we get it badly wrong and suffer consequential damage elsewhere or later downstream.

Our species is inherently attuned to simple tasks involving three or four variables. The crisis facing this planet involves hundreds of variables and we cannot be sure which are key, or how they are all interrelated. Planet Earth is a closed, not an open system. Moreover, we inherently think in a simple, linear and short-term way, while our world is inherently complex, chaotic, non-linear and long term.

Consider the impact of an AIDS programme that would potentially save millions from dying each year in Africa. Such a cure without effective

The big(gest) issues facing the planet and humanity?

- **Energy – Pollution – Ecosystem – Climate**
- **Raw materials availability**
- **Population – Migration**
- **Ageing – Healthcare**
- **Logistics – Transport – Constraints**
- **Education – Complexity – Understanding**
- **Political instability**

birth control would immediately give rise to food and water shortages and starvation would most likely follow. This is a cruel example of a simple interrelationship of a limited number of factors. Add to this the increased demand for fuel, housing and medicine, plus the spread of disease, and we have another human disaster in the making. It is insufficient to solve singular problems in a random order. The whole system has to be addressed, otherwise the solution could be far worse than the intended cure.

Unless we devote significant resources to creating models of the world in which we live, alongside the political and financial systems we employ, there is no chance that any world summit will have a positive impact on our trajectory. Only by some fortuitous stroke of luck could we select the right variables to affect and change the course on which we are set. Mother Nature on the other hand will do it for us without a thought – but we will most likely pay a terrible price. She offers no safeguards and no sympathy; she remorselessly obeys the laws of physics, and cares not for the suffering of any life form.

Personally I would prefer to make the effort to understand our overall situation and take action before we incur penalties from excess energy consumption, pollution and a disregard for those dying from disease and starvation. Many problems can be solved at modest expense, but others may cost us dearly today, and if not fixed the cost will be immeasurable further down the line.

It is hard to imagine how our leaders could think they have the necessary wisdom to sort out the world's problems without the aid of adequate models and machines. This is epitomized in the polarization and simplicity of thinking of those who say that the cause of the world's problems is a single factor such as past colonial regimes or multinationals. Conversely, I balk at the hawks who say we should burn the hydrocarbons and the planet will take care of itself. A visit to rapidly industrializing regions of the world is sufficient to worry any right-minded person about the pollution now being created.

Some problems are simple and have simple solutions. The problems facing humanity are not, and we have no idea how complex the solutions are. We need to invest time, money and computing power in order to find out – or we may worsen already desperate situations and conditions. The really good news is: we just about have the computational power to have a really good stab at this!

Byte 06
Counter-Intuitive Networks

In the GDP equation of any nation, the ability to move atoms and bits dominates productivity and ultimately dictates all primary wealth generation.

You don't have to engage in the design and construction networks for too long to become aware of their many operational and economic quirks. This is especially true of traffic behaviour when individual elements are afforded freedom of action. Bunching, waves and traffic jams turn out to be a naturally occurring phenomenon in all forms of network.

The result of self-determination in any networked population always has a similar outcome, whether the vehicles are cars, packets of bits on optical fibre, or the molecules of a gas in a pipe. What is difficult to forecast are all the generating mechanisms and the precise outcomes. One of the most common disrupters of mobile telecommunications is coffee, which brings widespread network chaos. The mechanism is delightful and centres on large conference gatherings. An audience is listening to the morning speaker and not making any calls, but when coffee arrives at 10:15am, hundreds of mobile phones demand network connection within seconds. Under these circumstances more often than not, the network cannot deliver. In the commuter sense it is more obvious. More people decide to travel into a city at the same time than the infrastructure can cope with. The knock-on effect of cancelled trains, road traffic accidents, and congestion, is the generation of even more clustered mobile phone calls!

There are only a limited number of options to improve the situation. For road traffic you can increase the throughput by adding extra lanes, adopt higher speed limits, and restrict or deter the number of vehicles accessing

Internet traffic density in the UK
Guess where all the people live!

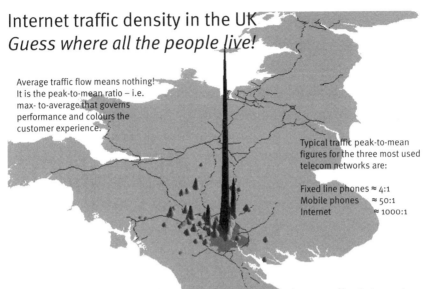

Average traffic flow means nothing!
It is the peak-to-mean ratio – i.e.
max- to-average that governs
performance and colours the
customer experience.

Typical traffic peak-to-mean
figures for the three most used
telecom networks are:

Fixed line phones ≈ 4:1
Mobile phones ≈ 50:1
Internet ≈ 1000:1

Population demographics, road traffic, telephone calls, Internet
access and GDP are all interrelated and fundamentally chaotic.

the road. Similarly for trains: you can only invest in more track, trains and carriages, try and spread the travel times of the customers, or employ faster trains, and of course deter people from travelling.

The use of IT as a travel substitute is an obvious release valve to remove some physical pressure, but it requires companies and people to change their work practices, and managers to grow up. Of course, many people are unable to apply remote working to any element of their job, so the overall change and impact is ultimately limited.

In every field of transport the degrees of freedom are always few and limited. Radical change and improvement generally mean new and revolutionary technology.

In the GDP equation of any nation, the ability to move atoms and bits dominates productivity and ultimately dictates all primary wealth generation. If people cannot get to work easily and they arrive tired and frustrated and have to leave early, then business suffers. If productivity is low, orders cannot be fulfilled and shipped, and if there are logistic delays, if meetings and decisions are also delayed by a lack of physical and bit bandwidth, then the GDP suffers. For example, the road, rail and air transport congestion in

Search engine –

chaotic search patterns and growth

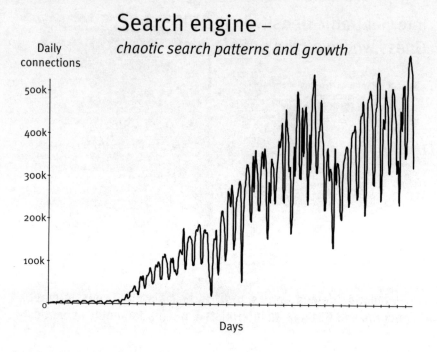

Daily connections

Days

the UK now costs far more than all the national investment in healthcare and education combined.

One thing is certain – all traffic problems, regardless of the mechanism they are created by, can be addressed, bounded and improved by design and investment. But very often the solutions are not so obvious and not so easy to engineer. Networks always seem to feature some level of counter-intuitive solution and outcome, but it is a topic that has received a good deal of study and we largely understand what has to be done to solve the problems. So, it is with some exasperation that I am sat in a traffic jam on the M25, listening to a government minister on the radio explaining that investment in roads and infrastructure will not improve the situation as it will encourage more cars onto the road, resulting in even more traffic jams.

In the UK there are 60M people in 20M homes with around 23M cars. Straight away it is clear that there are a finite number of cars and a finite number of drivers. Interestingly, and contrary to popular belief, cars don't always create and dominate traffic jams. Today it is predominately trucks and vans!

Another argument is that cars are detrimental to the environment because they create so much pollution and we should all migrate to public

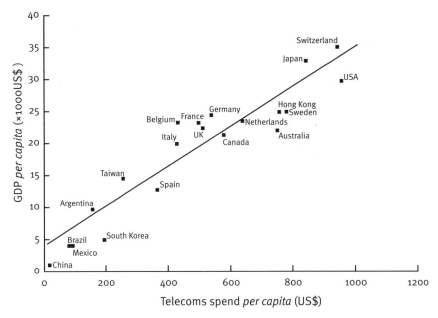

Source: Salomon Smith Barney

transport. Wrong again! Some 90% of all car journeys do not go from city centre to city centre, as do the train and bus services. Nor could the majority of journeys be completed by bus even when local. For the majority there is no alternative to the car. The reality is traffic jams cause pollution and not concrete roads. By restricting road-building programmes, pollution levels are increased not reduced! Static cars produce massive pollution; moving cars do not! It is journey time that is the all-important factor in the pollution equation. I would like to park my car in this particular minister's drive and leave the engine running for four hours every day, as that is what traffic jams are doing.

It is interesting that during this programme the argument quickly degenerates into political rhetoric and political correctness. At no point does anyone mention productivity and the effectiveness of the transportation network.

A few days before, I had attended a telecoms conference in the USA where the telcos where being harangued for installing too much fibre. Roughly speaking, they have a 40% overcapacity for the actual traffic demand. Again, I am amazed that no one has bothered to do the calculations. Fibre costs nothing compared to the civil engineering of installation. It makes no difference whether you install 1 fibre or 100, it is insignificant in the overall cost equation. In any case, the Internet is still growing at around 55% p.a. and this apparent overcapacity will be gone in 18 months. Just like roads, bandwidth and connectivity cost society nothing when compared to the losses in productivity.

We should be investing in integrated R&D programmes to realize improved transport systems. The focus should be to minimize the overall cost of moving goods and people on an individual basis over relatively short distances, with mass transportation between major cities and nodes. Unfortunately, while discontinuous and uneducated thinking remains, dominated by political agendas and non-holistic studies, we are going to be fed a diet of wrong conclusions and decisions. As far as I can see, a continuation of the transport chaos afflicting most of the planet is inevitable, and so are falling productivity levels. Perhaps we will soon make an even more obvious decision to start telecommuting as opposed to travelling. A looming oil crisis coupled with insignificant R&D investments in alternative energy sources could see us left with no choice – the ratio of true cost between physically travelling and telecommunications is generally $>> 100:1$.

Byte 07
Linear and Non-Linear

Almost all resource and logistics problems are inherently non-linear.

For years I have been trying to convey the key differences between a world that is linear and one that is not, to educated and lay audiences. In principle this seems a simple task, but it turns out to be incredibly difficult. The fact is that most of our education and worldly experience is founded on linear assumptions. From an early age we become conditioned to a majority experience that leads us to believe that linearity and order is the dominant condition, but the converse is true!

Of late I have been working with organizations that have always optimized their operations along traditional lines, with singular cost and performance parameters receiving all the attention. Without exception their single biggest mistake has been to optimize the individual components of a serial process, and then glue them together end-to-end as a complete system in the belief that the whole will then be optimal. But this is seldom the case! Only the simplest of systems behave in this way. Why?

Most of our experience with physical things and materials sees systems that are bounded and well behaved in controlled environments. For example, if we stretch an elastic band it will expand in direct proportion to the force being applied. If we go beyond 'the elastic limit' it will suffer damage and ultimately break. The same is true of wood, metals and plastics. Most of our design work is concerned with materials subjected to a given and limited tension or compression that will see them return to their original state after being flexed. We purposely concern ourselves with supporting structures that will not be damaged by vibration, such as the framework of a building, bridge or aircraft wing.

(A)   Systems and organizations of this type are linear if and only if every element is linear ...

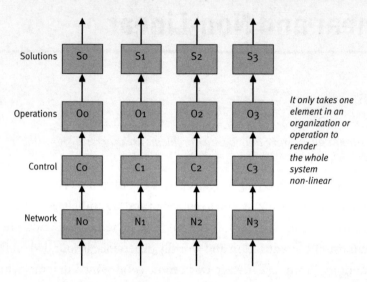

It only takes one element in an organization or operation to render the whole system non-linear

(B)   Systems and organizations of this type are inherently non-linear even if every element is linear and well behaved

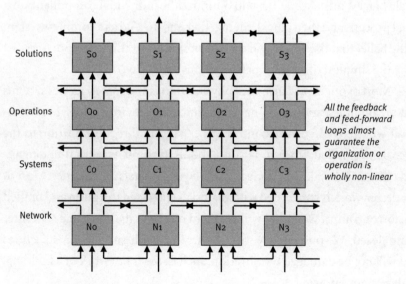

All the feedback and feed-forward loops almost guarantee the organization or operation is wholly non-linear

Simulation of six competing companies averaged over 30 trials

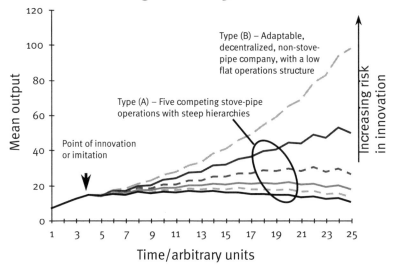

At school, college and university we focus on the well behaved so that theory and practice agree, and results can be repeated with the same apparatus by generation after generation of students. The non-linear aspects are only mentioned in passing, and then in terms of the catastrophic failure of deformation. And in many systems this is a sufficient view. Even the mathematicians are taken to solving the non-linear by the use of piece-wise linear approximations. But none of this prepares us for the non-linear conditions that increasingly confront us in real life.

If we were designing an automobile and wanted to make the drive chain as efficient as possible, we could work independently on the gear box to reduce the friction and optimize the gear ratios for acceleration and top speed and, similarly, the back axle and differential. We would ensure that the design of the engine gave maximum power for a given fuel consumption. When all were linked together to constitute the whole drive chain, it would indeed be optimum – providing a few issues of energy and torque matching have been taken care of.

This is an inherently linear system; the energy output varies in direct proportion to the energy input, given the losses due to frictional heating and noise. In a limiting case we could rev up the engine to the point where the materials overheat, extend beyond their normal limits, and then the system would become non-linear and irrevocably damaged. But the fundamental design assumes that all of the materials and the operation will be sustained within the limits of linear operation. This example is as good as any in terms of defining our linear thinking and approach to optimization.

So where does it all go wrong? Almost all resource and logistics problems are inherently non-linear. Probably one of the most graphic examples today would be the hospital bed manager in the UK or the bed marshal in the United States who are employed to achieve bed-fills in excess of 99%, which they do with great regularity. Unfortunately, this single point efficiency leads to an overall system inefficiency and is in itself a significant damage-generation mechanism.

The first effect is poor hygiene caused by a lack of time for bacteria to be cleared between bed occupancy. This leads to cross-infection between contiguous occupants, longer treatment times and patient return visits. Secondly, surgeons who would normally have all their patients on a single ward now have to locate them in wards and rooms randomly distributed across the entire hospital. In the worst cases patients may be moved from ward to ward on an almost daily basis. At this point overall surgeon and general medical staff productivity goes down. Thirdly, transport, administration, and overall operating costs escalate as medical records, patients and medics become disassociated. Of course, people become upset and dissatisfied as the inefficiency is all too obvious. The ticking time bomb in this scenario is that the hospital system is rendered unresponsive to any crisis of any scale. Any major disaster, such as an air crash, major road accident, or terrorist event, leads to chaos spanning many hospitals and road networks as patients and victims are transported to the nearest facility with available beds.

The really damaging outcome is that people die, don't get cured and become dependent upon long-term care. The overall system is made more inefficient, costs escalate, satisfaction goes down, politicians get involved and a downward spiral is invoked. The answer? Joined-up thinking! A full and all-encompassing analysis where the optimization is end-to-end, from start to finish, and not a single-point function.

I think I should make it plain that I am not singling out healthcare in particular. The observations are equally valid for transport systems – public and private, road and rail, containers and parcels, atoms and bits. Not to mention government, management, ecology, energy and living! Everywhere you look there are huge savings to be made by the application of deep thought, true understanding and effective models. Conversely, there are huge penalties for getting it wrong!

Byte 08

Exponential Growth – So Misunderstood

> *The real voyage of discovery consists not in seeking new landscapes but in having new eyes.*
>
> Marcel Proust

The economist Adam Smith was wrong. He was just too linear in his thinking.

There are two commonly misunderstood expressions used by the media and politicians that mildly amuse me for their inaccuracy. The first is quantum leap – which is, in fact, an infinitesimally small change. The second is exponential growth.

For the past three years I have been asking audiences of business leaders, planners, educators and politicians if they understand what an exponential function is? In an audience of 500 people, generally fewer than 10 people put up their hands and the rest admit that they do not really understand. Surprisingly, when I move on to explain that an exponential function is exactly like compound interest (what you pay on a loan or overdraft) I find that the vast majority still don't understand. They have a mortgage and a bank account, but they don't really understand compound interest and, therefore, exponential functions.

The function e^x (which = EXP(x) in computer speak) is so delightfully simple and so very deceptive! Here is a simple explanation. Suppose you work for me on the following basis: on day one I pay you \$2, on day two I pay you \$4, on day three \$8, day four \$16 and so on. How much will I pay you on the tenth day? The answer is \$1024. This is a counter-intuitive outcome, even more so on the twentieth day I will pay you slightly over \$1M and the thirtieth day slightly over \$1Bn. This is exponential growth.

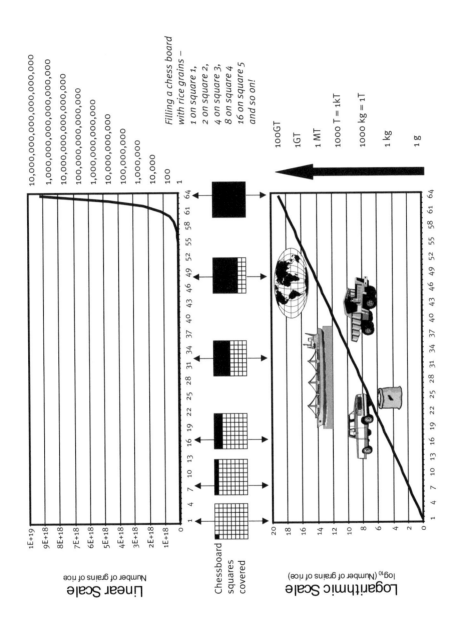

Filling a chess board with rice grains –
1 on square 1,
2 on square 2,
4 on square 3,
8 on square 4
16 on square 5
and so on!

1000 T = 1kT

1000 kg = 1T

100GT
1GT
1 MT
1 kg
1 g

Linear Scale
Number of grains of rice

10,000,000,000,000,000,000
1,000,000,000,000,000,000
10,000,000,000,000,000
100,000,000,000,000
1,000,000,000,000
10,000,000,000
100,000,000
1,000,000
10,000
100
1

1E+19
9E+18
8E+18
7E+18
6E+18
5E+18
4E+18
3E+18
2E+18
1E+18
0

Chessboard squares covered

Logarithmic Scale
$\log_{10}$ (Number of grains of rice)

20
18
16
14
12
10
8
6
4
2
0

Lets look at it another way – if you were to invest $1 at 10% interest compounded for ten years, you would receive $2.59, but if it were $1 for ten years at 100%, then you receive $1024.

An old conundrum says a king is asked to pay for work by placing a grain of rice on a square of a chessboard and then on day two, two grains, on the third, four grains and so on. By the last square of the chessboard the grains of rice will more than fill a castle, let alone a throne room. This also demonstrates how a viral infection rapidly becomes an epidemic – sneezing or skin contact is an exponential spreading mechanism! Say one person sneezing infects a further five, and then later they sneeze and infect another five, each giving a total 1 + 5 + 25, and so on. The same occurs with computer viruses that can now propagate around the planet in much less than a day via the Internet.

Starting on the 1st square with a single grain of rice, and doubling thereafter sees:

- over 9,000,000,000,000,000,000 grains on the last square of the board, and
- nearly 19,000,000,000,000,000,000 covering the entire board area.

The total weight of the rice grains on the chessboard is approximately 100Gt or 100,000,000,000 metric tonnes. *This equates to the combined weight of around 400,000 of the biggest oil tankers on the planet. By weight and volume it is greater than the annual rice production of our planet*

Probably the most frightening exponential experience would be to sit on a beach and notice a wave on the horizon, but by the time you realize it is a tsunami it is too late to run. You will be swallowed up by the advancing wave and die. Yes – perception can be exponential too! The ground rush when you land a plane or drop by parachute are both examples of non-linear exponential perception. One minute you are relaxed, the next in panic!

Driving a car at great speed sees a similar distortion of our perception and we become unbelievably tolerant and confident on an open road. Only when we pull onto the off-ramp do we suddenly perceive that we are travelling extremely fast and everything suddenly happens in an apparently very much shorter time.

- *From a single human cell only 47 divisions (doublings) create a 70kg adult.*
- *Just 42 divisions create a newborn child – and just 5 more an adult.*
- *This, of course, is the base case, and we have to add the absorption of fat and water.*

Technology follows the same exponential laws, and the change it engenders may appear to be insignificant and on the horizon, but by the time it is perceived as a threat it is often too late. Moore's Law is the most celebrated exponential law in the IT industry. It accurately predicted that integrated circuit density, and hence computer power, would double in power every 12–18 months from 1960 onwards. There are other, similar laws for optical fibre bandwidth, network capacity, hard-drive storage, and so on. In fact it is difficult to find anything in IT that isn't governed by an exponential growth in capability and an exponential fall in cost/price.

The 'S' curve continuum

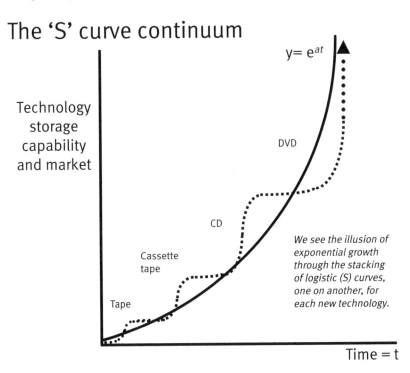

Technology storage capability and market

$y = e^{at}$

DVD

CD

Cassette tape

Tape

We see the illusion of exponential growth through the stacking of logistic (S) curves, one on another, for each new technology.

Time = t

Internet hosts (linear scale)

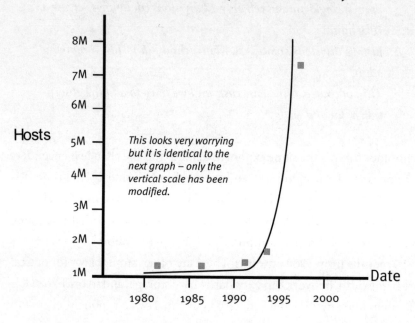

This looks very worrying but it is identical to the next graph – only the vertical scale has been modified.

Same data – showing exponential growth – in both figures

Internet hosts (log scale)

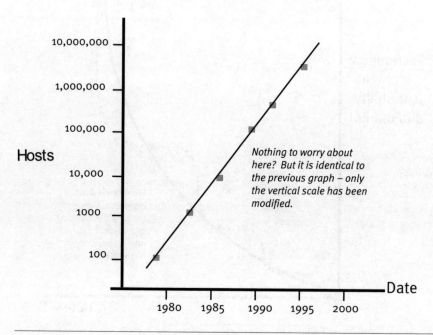

Nothing to worry about here? But it is identical to the previous graph – only the vertical scale has been modified.

Chip cost-performance doubles every 18 months (Moore's Law)

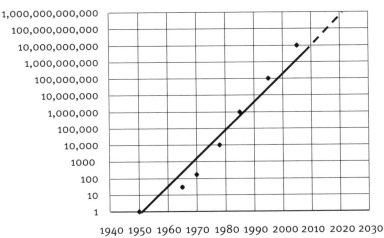

Cooper's law for wireless

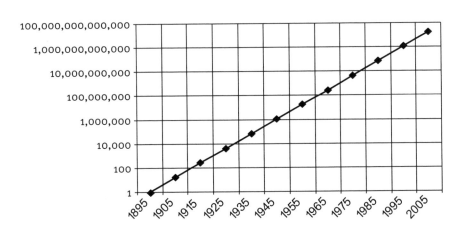

The number of conversations (voice and data) has doubled every 2½ years since 1895

Adam Smith was wrong in his own time and he is even more in error today. In his economic model of the universe there is a finite source of material with limited production, routes to market, finance and communication. People can only afford to buy a limited amount of furniture, clothing, food and luxury goods. And so the finite supply of raw materials, production capability, coupled with a limited number of supply channels, leads to essentially well-behaved and understandable markets. This results in a *linear channel* model of economics with a finite population of limited appetite, expectation and money, a limited supply of materials and goods, and a finite number of channels between the two. This was a model that worked well when the world was a slow-moving place, but not today – we are moving much faster!

It is now apparent that in a bit-based economy the source of raw materials (bits) is unlimited in terms of production, routes to market, finance and communication. There is no limit to what customers will purchase and use or expect and communicate. We have an insatiable appetite for music, movies, games, photographs, and publications of all kinds – professional and amateur. Furthermore, we are all now linked by highly non-linear channels involving fixed and mobile networks, telephones, email, fax, radio, TV and computers, plus people networks of travellers who span the planet.

What is the big deal here? We have evolved to think in terms of, and deal with, essentially linear problems and situations. So it is perhaps not surprising that we are mostly wrong-footed by the exponential and non-linear. I suspect that we don't do anyone any favours by trying to make the exponential more palatable by the use of logarithmic scales on all our scientific, engineering and economic plots. These just straighten out the growth line and present a comforting linear distortion. Convenient it might be, but very deceptively so! Without a fundamental grasp of the math involved it is difficult to convey to anyone how serious a function this is. The depletion of raw materials, use of energy, destabilization of weather patterns, and the onset of war are but a few of the more catastrophic scenarios subject to e^x.

How different all this is to even 100 years ago, when most things appeared linear and well behaved – and how dangerous when planners, politicians, decision makers and leaders do not understand the most fundamental of functions that now governs the growth of trade, communication, wealth and risk.

Adam Smith...et al (1723–1790)
3/4D thinking

Finite source of atoms

Linear channel

Finite sink user appetite

Physical stores and a very slow supply chain

Limited:
- materials
- production
- routes to market
- finance
- communication

Limited:
- population
- appetites
- expectation
- finance
- communication

Today
nD – non-linear thinking

Infinite source of bits

Non-linear channel/s

Infinite sink user appetite

Limited:
- bits
- production
- routes to market
- finance
- communication

Physical stores, virtual stores, multiple devices, routes, contacts, and a very fast supply chain

Limited:
- population
- appetites
- expectation
- finance
- communication

Byte 09
Don't Make Life Harder Than It Already Is

A lesson for everyone – especially debt-laden telcos … Could it be that principal players have misread a world increasingly making use of simple, DIY solutions …?

As a child I had considerable problems gaining an education. Not that anyone denied me the opportunity – no one tried to stop me, I just didn't seem to fit. Or rather my brain didn't. It was hard for me not to think and always ask 'Why?' The system demanded a blind acceptance of fact and function – just learn all this stuff because that's the way it is.

My struggle with education continued throughout my time at university. Always asking why, digging deeper and trying to understand seemed a necessity to me. Even during my decades in R&D I solved problems by thinking differently rather than blindly turning handles. In my later years in industry, my solutions always seemed different to the norm and not straight out of any textbook.

When asked to join a large team and build my initial R&D budget I watched fellow managers counting the pencils and paper, people and equipment, spending days building the numbers a line at a time, bottom up. To their disconcert I went to the Fortune 500 and looked at the total earnings per company, number of employees and amount of R&D budget. I then calculated the average earnings and expenditure per employee and estimated the standard deviation.

Interestingly, when the managers submitted all the numbers, they were all in the same ballpark. In my case I had spent my spare days working on the detail of my programme and the recruiting of staff. My rationale said that creating an R&D budget has been done thousands of times by thousands of managers – and perhaps I could ride on their wisdom and efforts. Well, it worked!

People employed by a Telco

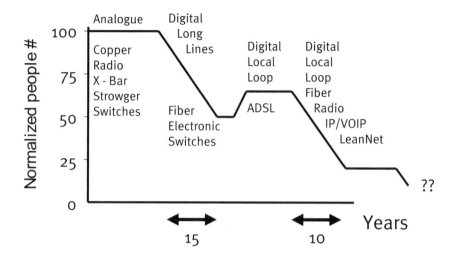

More recently I was looking at the recovery forecasts and rhetoric being put forward by leaders and managers in the telecoms sector. From fixed line to mobile there is a good deal of positive spin that I find hard to support. I don't think broadband or 3G will save them – quite the contrary.

While the analysts and gurus present their deep and complex models for this sector, it can be as simple as this: take a large sample of the leading telcos and add up their current debts. It is easy to get to $500Bn. Then add up the post-tax, pre-crash profits for the same group and the number comes out around $100Bn. Then look at the declared pre- and post-crash capital expenditure (capex) of each company and it averages much less than 50%. Next, take a look at profitability, and that is way down too.

What can we gather from these numbers? First, there is no way this group of companies can recover their position in less than five years – dividing $500Bn by $100Bn gives us that figure straight away.

Second, the fall in profits and capex says their expansion into broadband, 3G and all the associated money-making services being put forward as the next big thing are going to be severely limited unless they can muster novelty and help from outside the sector. And worse, broadband in particular poses a self-inflicted threat as it can be used to support Internet

Eventually everything becomes...
... a commodity

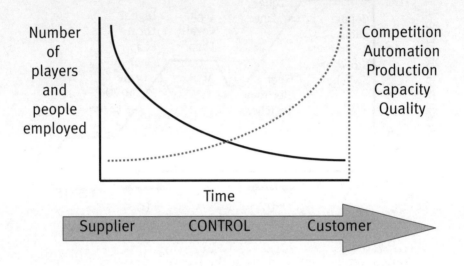

Eventually everything becomes...
... a commodity

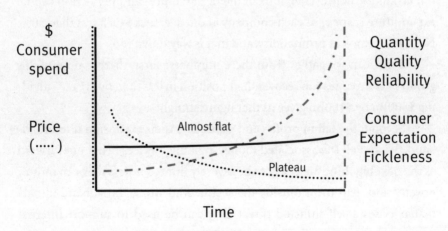

Telephony (VOice over IP – VOIP). This potentially allows all broadband customers to bypass the telephone network and thereby reduce the income and profitability of the phone companies even further and faster.

Inside the companies themselves, and away from the public eye, the word is hunker down, sweat the assets, run down service levels, talk up the value, project a positive face and talk recovery. But in the boardrooms the talk is of merger and consolidation, of cost reduction and staffing levels. Tough times indeed.

My forecast is for a seven-to-ten year recovery with a massive reduction in the number of companies and people, with little investment in appropriate infrastructure that would actually make a long-term difference. I suspect we will see the quiet abandonment of a lot of copper-based broadband services, and the gradual demise of an already badly wounded 3G effort. At best I see an accelerated slow down, across a broad front.

In the same way, food, automotive and electronics production have made one-way transitions before, I don't expect the telecoms sector to recover its former gloss and profitability 100%. The recent damage done by the dot-com bust, economic downturn and WorldCom scandal etc., has not only tarnished the image of telcos, it has seen an important transition to a sector of narrow margins and oblique competition. The economy of this planet cannot afford hundreds of network companies. It can only support a handful.

So where will the new growth come from? I was in Fry's Electronics (Palo Alto) recently and saw 180GB hard drives for $120 and the price of PCs and laptops seemingly around 70% of 12 months ago. I also saw mountains of WiFi (IEEE 802.11) wireless networking equipment being sold for home and office use at prices spanning $50–$150. The rate of sale was awesome!

I suspect the pent-up demand for wideband (not broadband) is growing and isn't going away. If the network companies cannot supply, I think the population at large will engineer and supply it themselves. We've seen similar examples of users going it alone in the past 50 years. In particular the growth of self-install Community Antenna TV systems proved the only viable way far-flung communities in the mid-west of the USA could economically get access to a TV signal in the 1940/50s. In later decades these networks went commercial and became part of the cable TV industry. Could it be that DIY nets are 'go' yet again and history is about to repeat itself? If *yes*, we could see slim pickings for the traditional operators!

People expect to install their own TV, hi-fi, PC, LAN and WiFi – so why not their own section of the first/last mile?

Connection cost

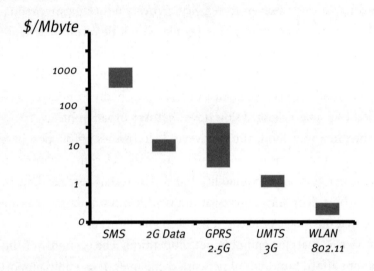

Byte 10

The 3G Chasm – Deeper Than We Thought

Some governments chose to give away 3G spectrum licences. Others ran auctions at the height of the tech bubble, raising billions along the way. Who was wisest?

It has always amazed me that corporations will stare reality in the face and still make stupid decisions. The notion that people spending an average of $50 per month on their mobile phone will suddenly increase that spend fivefold when they move to 3G beggars belief. Disposable income tends to be almost constant for most people – and an increase on anything means robbing the budget elsewhere. It is almost impossible for most people to earn more money – especially for dubious luxuries.

As a prime example I can cite my digital camera. Since the arrival of the first digital cameras I have been an avid user. My principle spend has been on the cameras themselves, which I seem to change and update about every 18–24 months, along with my laptop. What I don't do is buy film for wet processing anymore, but my expenditure has remained almost uniform over time because of the batteries I buy. To be precise, my past expenditure on 35mm film has been replaced by expenditure on batteries. The real upside is that I now get ten times as many pictures per $. I think variants of this model also apply to most sectors of IT – we just keep getting more for less, and thereby squeeze more out of the same pot of money – disposable income for IT just keeps stretching.

People have a fixed amount of disposal income and a subconscious comfort level for the $ allocation per activity. It is universally difficult for them to put more into the pot. If the telecoms sector is to get more money out of each household, office and mobile phone it has to be taken away

Consumer spending is defined by total disposable income...
they can only divert it from one sector to another...
there is no new money!

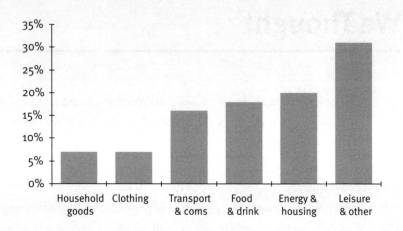

Applications are critical

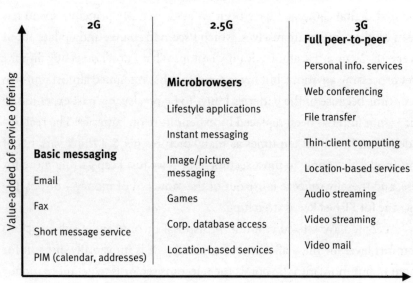

2G	2.5G	3G Full peer-to-peer
		Personal info. services
	Microbrowsers	Web conferencing
	Lifestyle applications	File transfer
	Instant messaging	Thin-client computing
Basic messaging	Image/picture messaging	Location-based services
Email		Audio streaming
Fax	Games	Video streaming
Short message service	Corp. database access	Video mail
PIM (calendar, addresses)	Location-based services	

Value-added of service offering

Bandwidth required to support applications

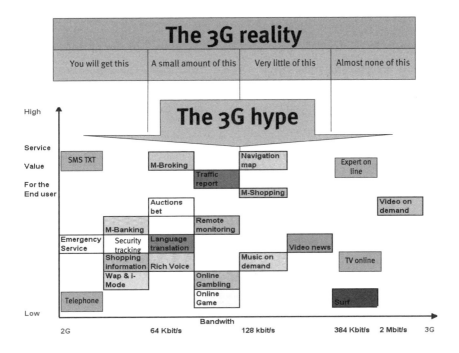

from some other sector. On one level it is obvious how this can be done, but it needs different sectors to cooperate and change the way they work and trade.

One obvious partner would be the music industry which is under severe attack from Napster/Kazaa-like services where people can download MP3 files and bypass the entire production, sales, marketing and delivery chain. Countries such as Germany and the US, which have among the most advanced broadband programmes on the planet, saw a fall of 5–15% in CD sales by mid 2002. The UK, which has a less aggressive broadband programme, saw a 5% fall in CD sales early in 2003. In North America the figures are even more dramatic and a copyright war is in full swing.

The new opportunity is for people to purchase music and download over a broadband connection to a PC, or directly to a mobile phone encapsulating an MP3 player. This also means that a large percentage of the new IT money would be extracted from the music industry. Interestingly, the music industry seems unable to adapt to this threat. It seems a technology and business model too far – and means closing down CD production facilities and changing the distribution and royalty models.

We have only to look at our now lengthy telecommunications and IT history to see why the present difficulties prevail in the mobile sector. Without exception, every single service and money-making concept has been exceptionally simple and, for the most part, trivial. The vast majority of telephone calls and certainly almost all of the SMS text messages that are now sent constitute very little value in terms of contribution to society and humanity's progress. For the individual, the trivia they communicate is important and on a very social level, so they are prepared to pay for it.

Meanwhile, in the research labs of the planet our best minds are focused on creating services for 3G telephones that no one is likely to purchase. These include wonderful services such as being able to locate the nearest restaurant with a table free at a particular time and read the menu, or being called by the nearest store to hear that they have that jacket you have been looking for in stock and in your size. I suspect that such services have little to offer real users and probably no chance of success in the market.

Something really trivial, like building a small camera into a mobile phone so that young people can take photographs of friends and transmit them from one side of the planet (or restaurant) to the other, is far more likely to take off. But only if the price is right – it has to be almost free!

Without a healthy telecommunications and IT sector we will all suffer. With an ongoing spend on 3G that is tantamount to pouring money down the drain I can see operators being in debt for some considerable time. I estimate this as follows: across the industry operators have an average debt mountain of the order of five years of their pre-crash, post tax profits. This has been created by the removal of over $100Bn by governmental rape of the industry, compounded by $100Bn spend budget for new infrastructure, plus another $100Bn required for the production of handsets, deployment, marketing and sales.

My financially based estimate is that the mobile companies will take five to seven years (from 2000) to climb out of a huge hole they largely dug for themselves. The impact on the rest of IT and telecommunications will be severe. I suspect that this once most vigorous and vital of industries has not only stalled, but has actually downturned permanently, never to return to the golden days we have seen over the past 20 years.

In 2001 I predicted that companies would close, and operators would have to merge, and 250,000 people would be put out of work across the EU by greedy governments. Unfortunately I was right, and I think we have yet to see the end game! More operational consolidation, outsourcing, staffing and OPEX reductions are on the cards along with some interesting prospects for WLANs and 4G.

The 3G debacle was a bad mistake, and it has left a big hole to fill!

Byte 11
Science and Belief

The business world would do well to learn from the kind of verification and peer group review that is central to science.

I can't recall the point in my education and training when I became so enamoured by the scientific method, but a lifelong exposure over many projects has made me a strong advocate. What has been surprising is the difficulty that I, and others, experience in trying to explain and defend the inherent power and surety of science to those outside the community.

As a student I had the good fortune to have professors who insisted I solved problems using at least three different techniques, starting with different assumptions, to achieve the same answer. When the same or very similar answers to a given problem were realized in this manner, only then could we be confident we were on the right track. However, at the leading edge of science, engineering and business we often find ourselves with a very limited scenario of options and we may be lucky to find even one solution. The techniques and starting conditions available are often dictated by limited choices and incomplete solutions and understanding.

Ultimately we rely upon the practical experiment, theoretical and computer modelling, of many others independently achieving the same or similar results. In an ideal world, experimenters should be free of bias in their selection of technique, measurement and subject. When involving human subjects, they too should be unaware of what is being done, how it is being done, and what the outcome might be. All theoretical expectation and predisposition has to be taken out for a conclusive result. And very often the outcomes turn out to be counter-intuitive! This is the discovery and verification process that has seen our species progress so rapidly and surely over the last 500 years.

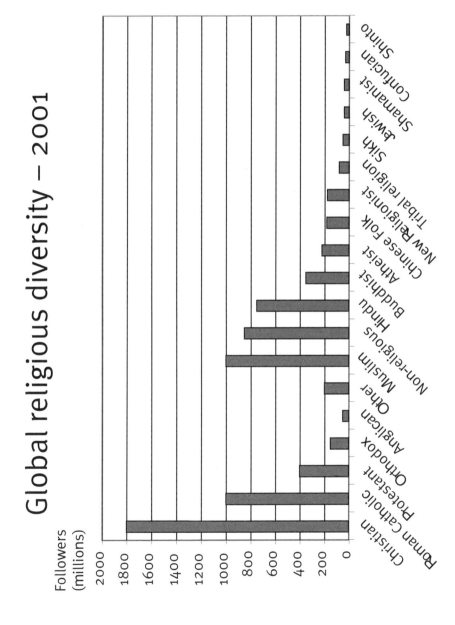

Global religious diversity – 2001

Belief systems

The 2001 edition of Barrett's *World Christian Encyclopaedia* identifies 10,000 distinct religions. Of these, 150 have a million or more followers. Christianity has 33,830 different denominations ranging from Catholicism as the largest, to Shakers as one of the smallest.

Most religions tend to be concentrated in particular geographical regions, and are often a defining character of particular ethnic groups. There are 22 religions with a significant presence beyond a single country or area; these are considered the major world religions.

The most successful disbelief system ever! The scientific method

1   Observe a phenomenon or pose a question
2   Form a hypothesis and/or theory
3   Build a model and/or conduct an experiment
4   Test (2 and 3) and establish closeness of fit with (3)
5   Repeat/refine (2–4) many times to establish repeatability and confidence
6   Publish/communicate results to the scientific community
7   Subsume peer review/criticism from (6)
8   Subsume supporting (or otherwise) results by other teams
9   Agree a consensus view over as wide a population as possible
10   Continually review in the light of related developments
11   Be prepared to revisit and further refine

In the case of testing drugs, for example, it is best that the clinicians involved have no idea whether they are administering a given drug or placebo, and the same should apply to the patients. The real experimenters are the observers who play no part in the administration or the measurement. When this is repeated in at least three different locations across the planet, and a good result correlation has been achieved, then and only then are they deemed credible.

Ideally, practitioners and patients should be blind to the experiment, and the observers analysing the outcomes should be the only people aware of all the variables. This 'double blindness' is the most powerful safeguard we have devised to guard against human fallibility, bias, preconception and graft.

This approach turns out to be our ultimate method of establishing the truth over belief and achieving real understanding. We also employ publishing to make all techniques and results public, and then others can repeat and confirm or criticize our experiments, and continue to refine and polish techniques, theories and models. Not surprisingly, a large percentage of experiments tend to be unrepeatable in the wider scientific community and therefore the results are dismissed or parked for later investigation. And, in the case of Einstein, 'later' turned out to be 50 years. So the world can get by on just a theory, but it makes us so much more comfortable when verified by experimentation!

Such a gatekeeper function is of immense value, as it guards against fraud, human error, bigotry, personal bias, greed and blind belief. These safeguards are essential in science, engineering and technology as all advance by standing on the shoulders of previous generations and their assured results. If we do not build our knowledge in this way, we will be creating a house of cards standing on a foundation of sand.

Outside the reaches of science we find a multiplicity of belief systems and practices leading to wrong assumptions, decisions and, very often, catastrophes. In the past few years, for example, we have seen the accounting profession discredited in the shape of Andersen Consulting, Enron and WorldCom – plus many more since! According to press reports, the US Generally Accepted Accounting Principles (GAAP) were flouted, cross checks ignored, and results massaged and interpreted for reasons essentially down to human greed and/or ignorance. The management cross checks that were in place were either flouted, ignored, or omitted by accident or design. This really was a systems failure that allowed multiple crimes on a scale never witnessed before.

Legal and governmental systems are also prone to promote grief as they too are dominated by human fallibility rather than rigorous and testable frameworks. We see governments adjusting figures to show improvements in education and healthcare year on year to appease an electorate.

But very quickly a few percentage point improvements year on year leads to an unbelievable state of disparity between the political mirage and practical experience. The downside of such trust violations centre on the raised expectation of the individual and society, ultimately followed by a loss of value and credibility. In short, the currency becomes devalued!

Unfortunately the same is true in many circles of human activity and is deeply embedded in all management, social, political and religious systems. Individuals choose to ignore demand, technology, human nature, practical and theoretical evidence and experience. Why? Belief systems, human ignorance, stupidity and vested interests are powerful allies and extremely resilient in all cultures, past and present. It is often more convenient, or even palatable, to live with something false than to deal with the truth.

If education and training systems are improving as advertised, we should be witnessing huge improvements in governance and decision-making, but I suspect all are getting worse. How come? Fewer people are being educated to appreciate any form of science and, as a result, the concept of system and operational consequences is being lost. Worse still, technology is widely regarded by more and more as some form of magic, and being technologically and scientifically ignorant has become fashionable.

The real downside to all of this is that in an IT-dominated world that is moving faster, and becoming increasingly non-linear, belief systems are even more damaging. Bad decisions now create even worse results in a much shorter time than they did 10 or 20 years ago.

Byte 12
Cochrane's Law of Secretaries

Three people rarely do three times the work of one person doing the
same job. Will the wired economy change that?

In those labour-intensive days before the PC and office automation, I had
the experience of working with a number of secretaries and assistants in
large offices. On each occasion when I started a new operation it would
involve me, a secretary and perhaps an assistant. We would build the business, gain orders, recruit people and create an organization to satisfy a given
demand.

At some point I would have to engage additional office staff and
then I would begin to notice a very definite and clear effect in terms of the
real work output. This I called 'Cochrane's Law of Secretaries', and it went
roughly like this:

- 1 secretary = 1 secretary's output
- 2 secretaries = 1.8 secretaries' output
- 3 secretaries = 2.6 secretaries' output
- 4 secretaries = 3.3 secretaries' output
- And so on!

It always seemed to be the case that putting extra people into the same work
area merely levelled off the work output to some asymptote with the total
number employed. This is sometimes referred to as the 'painters in a room'
problem. You can employ more painters to paint a room and get the job
done faster, but eventually there are so many painters they can't all get to the
wall and start to apply paint to each other.

Collective people IQ

In most office and admin environments the best you can hope for is a people effectiveness/work output/IQ that grows as $\sqrt{n}$

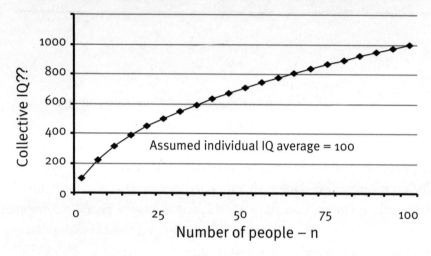

Most definitely ten secretaries don't do ten secretaries' work. It seems a basic human need and desire to talk, communicate and interact, and this becomes amplified by the added complexity of an organization that is growing. In an office environment we quickly see an increasing amount of time dissipated or distracted by other activities best defined as socializing work and processes. As work becomes more complex, more networked and faster, the communication overhead required in a strictly human-to-human network grows rapidly and takes individuals' energy from the primary purpose.

I am not picking on secretaries in particular you understand. This is a general condition that has parallels with the behaviour of other large groups. Over the years I have noticed this condition or 'law' to be true of administrations in general or indeed almost any group employed in a highly interactive environment. Ultimately, more becomes less for the old modes of working.

On another plane I have also observed a more damaging aspect. If ten people start a new company with a single administrator, it is clear that admin is there to support the nine in the creation of the company, finding customers, realizing orders and achieving profitability. This set up applies for some time as the company grows to 100, 500, 1000 and so on. But at

Smart people – dumb company

In reality effectiveness/work output/IQ tends to top out, decline and plateau. But, in the worst case, it can become destructive!

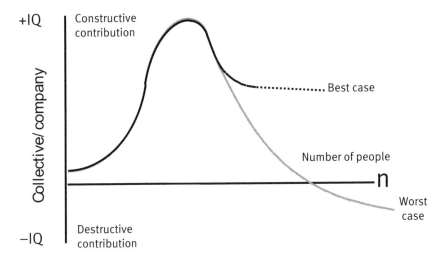

some point the value and belief system get inverted and the administration becomes the means to an end. Divorced from customers, markets, finance and personnel they become the core of the company and the rest are there to support them. This condition is dangerous and often fatal, with death engendered by a growing lack of customer awareness and increasing insulation from reality, usually compounded by a focus of effort on nonsense activities, fact gathering, analysis and erroneous decisions.

I'm not sure there is a 100% modern equivalent to all this. We now see companies virtualized, distributed and networked, with huge numbers of people chatting on email, instant messaging, sending text messages and talking on the telephone as opposed to being involved in discussions across the desk or via pieces of paper. The best managers no longer broadcast and dictate but communicate, create and support. Everyone can see the company condition via electronic access to constantly updated briefings and databases.

Another general observation about the eBusiness world: our work output tends to increase roughly tenfold every ten years but without a complete dissipation of individuals' energy in socializing work.

It is clear that similar laws apply to the overall intelligence of organizations in general. I tend to think of this in terms of corporate IQ. In short, the IQ or smartness of an organization does not appear to go hand in hand with the number of people employed. Often it is quite the reverse. It is not unusual to find very smart people employed in apparently very dumb organizations or, alternatively, very smart people creating very dumb organizations.

In engineering and science there is a very well known and common phenomenon often referred to as coherence. In brief, if two coherent signals or forces are added together they do so arithmetically, so: $3 + 4 = 7$. But when they are incoherent they tend to add on a power basis giving $SQRT(3^2 + 4^2) = SQRT(9 + 16) = SQRT(25) = 5$.

This also seems to be a fair approximation of what happens with our mental capability. It would appear the best you can hope for is that two people are jointly $SQRT(1^2 + 1^2) = SQRT(2) = 1.4 \times$ smarter. If the number of people increases, then the effective IQ seems to rapidly level off, well before the total equals 100 people. The exception – if there really is one – is when we restrict team sizes and network all the participants in a company or on a project.

The next big step is going to be the inclusion of smart machines, and the big question is whether they will follow the same limiting laws. I suspect not, as their communication, socializing and apportionment of work is without emotion or human frailty – they will just get on with it.

Byte 13
Control Freaks – Scales of Grey

When to be a control freak, when to let creativity flourish ...

During my decades in industry I observed people struggle with organizational structure and management methods. Broadly speaking, when a company gets into some difficulty the board will call in the consultants. The consultants trawl the company, talking to people to find out what they think, and put together a report that broadly reflects everyone's thoughts. *There is nothing like telling the customer what they want to hear to ensure that you get the next contract!*

The usual outcome of one of these very expensive exercises is simple. If the company happens to be centralized in its management and decision-making, the consultants will advise a break-up, to move to distributed management control and finance. If, however, the consultants discover the company is fully distributed, they will immediately propose centralization as the answer. Over a period of time you will see corporations imitating a concertina as they go in and out, from centralized to distributed and back again.

It has become increasingly apparent that the primary reason for continual reorganization has been the inadequacy of management structures and techniques in a world that is changing faster, where competition can come from any sector and where managers move from one job to another like butterflies. Every time a new CEO arrives he or she is duty-bound to do something because the CEO has to be seen to be effective. As a general rule, such rapid change is not good and usually leads to significant damage to companies and their employees.

Interval between an innovation and competitive entry

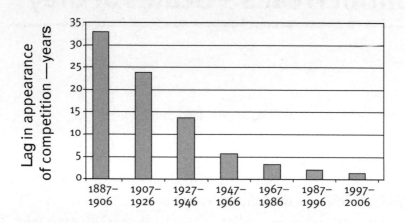

The reality is that management techniques and structures being used today are right out of the 19th century and more akin to a world of Charles Dickens than a world of 21st-century technology. They are rigid, hierarchical and fundamentally unsuited to a technologically driven world. And, worse, at every economic downturn or hiccup the battle cry is always back to basics, stick to the knitting, stop thinking, stop being creative, and cut all investment and operating costs. No Nobel Prizes here for novelty!

Let's examine two extremes of business. Suppose we have a huge manufacturing operation that is in the business of assembling automobiles. In fact, nobody manufactures automobiles today. The plants and the companies have become the systems integrators. Components are harvested from all over the planet, brought together in one plant, and with a unique set of jigs, fixtures and design capability, automobiles are assembled.

In such a plant there is a place for hierarchy, for all must be known and ordered. The design, construction and performance of every element are well understood and documented. The last thing required on any production line is uncontrolled innovation – it would jeopardize everything. Leave well alone and maintain throughput and quality has to be the focus.

Centralize or decentralize?

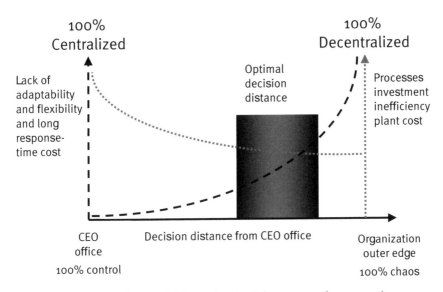

This arena is about yield, getting it right over and over again – non-stop. Whether it be computer hard drives, washing machines, television sets or automobiles on the production line, yield is the key. In such organizations it is not unusual to find between four and ten levels of management. It works, and it is necessary. Everyone has to have a clearly defined role and know precisely what they're about. This is a well-ordered regime where everything runs like clockwork.

The second example is the research organization where absolutely nothing is defined apart from a general direction of trying to create solutions. In industrial research, people are generally aware that they are employed to find solutions to known problems. In other cases they are involved in the creation of new technology to reduce costs of existing solutions, or the creation of something new that we have yet to imagine. In such an operation, hierarchy is a killer. Nothing is defined and little is known apart from the general direction.

In a research organization, strong leadership is required. Marshalling the brains of a multitude of PhDs is about harder than trying to herd cats. Investigations are initiated, paths are searched – and the vast majority are dead-ends. But search they must and explore they have to, as nobody knows the correct course and there are always surprises.

Lasers, for example, spent over 30 years as a solution looking for a problem and today they are manufactured like jelly beans as vital parts in DVD/CD drives and optical fibre systems. Until the 1970s no one had a use for coherent light but we may well see lasers employed to create quantum devices that operate very close to absolute zero to give us computational power beyond our wildest imagination.

In such endeavours, research needs hierarchy like a scientist needs a hole in the head. A hierarchy of two – leader–manager–people – is generally adequate and necessary. A steeper hierarchy just disables the operation because it brings out the control freak. This is the type of person who wants to know exactly how money is being spent, right down to every pencil, and what the outcome and benefit has been.

There is no doubt about it, research is a wasteful operation and it is often difficult to quantify the final outcome. But when optical fibres were first being drawn and lasers were first being developed and management/ finance were complaining of the outrageous expenditure for zero return, none of them had 0.1% of the necessary imagination to see a world powered by light and dominated by IT.

Modern companies are finding it increasingly difficult to muster the tolerance across the spectrum required to host all aspects of their past operations...

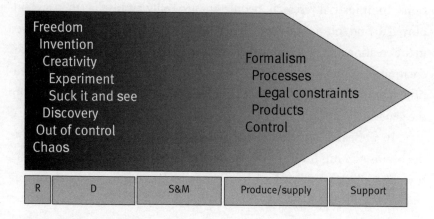

Somewhere on that span of the hierarchical spectrum sit people who have to make difficult decisions on the basis of often incomplete information. It is apparent they will have to become much more flexible in their approach and that the coexistence of manufacturing and research, and all activities in between, is going to be increasingly difficult. The most likely outcome is more outsourcing on these scales of grey as the coexistence of widely differing cultures in one organization as the technology makes them ever more visible. So R&D looks like being increasingly outsourced from operations as our technology progresses.

The current trend in most companies is to disband and outsource all R&D in order to focus on customer services and making money. But without adequate investment in R&D there will be no future services or technologies. I think we have a broken model and are witnessing a reorganization of resources, a polarization along an axis of order and chaos. Ultimately this could prove to be far more effective as R&D becomes more holistic and eclectic, and less constrained. The only criticality is the final scale of the operations – they have to achieve a critical mass to be effective and sustainable.

Byte 14
ButterflyWings.com

A butterfly flaps its wings and a dot-com goes bust?
Chaos theory is a phrase commonly bandied around, but have you
ever considered the various factors that led to the Internet bubble?

Apart from the occasional ice age or natural disaster such as a hurricane, earthquake or tsunami, our species has enjoyed a reasonably stable and linear existence. We have evolved appropriately to appreciate three spatial dimensions and one time dimension, with a sense of past, present and future. Most of us think in such terms and do not step into a world that exhibits ten or more dimensions, and yet all of our modern business and commerce problems tend to be multidimensional, and therefore well beyond our natural ability to grasp as a whole.

Everything in nature is multidimensional, non-linear and chaotic. From the clustering of the constellations in the night sky to weather, lightning storms and the evolution of life itself, all are governed by chaotic mechanisms. For any life to be successful it has to live on the edge of death. For you and me, our hearts are always close to fibrillation, and if they are not, then they wouldn't work and we would be dead.

At a more prosaic level, we see people in our families being born, getting married and dying in clusters; we see our domestic appliances failing at the same time; and we see car accidents clustered in twos and threes. All of the mechanisms involved revolve about a very similar wear out, repair and replace cycle, applicable to life forms and technology alike!

Perhaps more evidently the occurrence of chaos is really visible on road networks. It isn't by accident that you can stand and wait for a taxi or a bus for 20 minutes, not see one, then five or six come at once. It is not by accident that on motorways the traffic naturally bunches and comes in clusters. It turns out to be a fundamental result of any system that sees intelligent entities making independent decisions based on the actions of others.

How come chaos is generally unrecognized and has not been noticeably reported or deemed significant until very recently? It is all down to speed and perception. One hundred years ago the chaos of the world passed us by. Our frame of life was short compared to occurrence of chaotic events. Today, speed of communication and physical travel are making our lifetime perceptibly much longer and therefore chaotic events are becoming very noticeable.

The recent dot-com crash is a good example of a situation that has occurred many times before, the most recent being the Industrial Revolution. In the year 1900 there were more than 1000 manufacturers of automobiles in the US. By 1930 there were four. The Industrial Revolution spanned a 100-year time period, thousands and thousands of companies were created, but only a few survived. In the dot-com world that's exactly what happened in less than ten years.

In a linear world we have always looked at a vast field of variables or influencing factors in a situation, picked out the three or four most visible items, and analysed and assessed the situation. We have then made a deci-

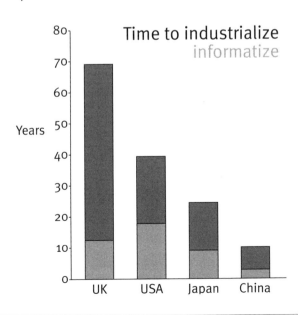

Time is the enemy...

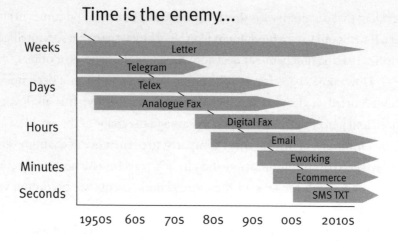

sion on that basis which often results in a single number answer, or a simple yes/no decision.

Incredibly, this simple-minded linear approach has served us well and resulted in most of our key advances and achievements. But that kind of approach, that kind of logic, can now lead to massive failures. We are talking butterfly wings causing an economic hurricane. In a predominantly non-linear and chaotic world a small perturbation can cause a massive change. This is now a world where some insignificant parameter or factor that we choose to overlook is actually very significant and can have dire consequences.

In 1986, the London Stock Market took the first of several steps towards fully automated trading for many functions. Unfortunately the systems and software employed had very similar decision thresholds (for buy and sell etc.). So when the market switched from manual (human) to automatic (machine) operation it immediately went into a limit cycle of alternate buy and sell. The fast networks linking the machines ensured that all communication and decision delay had been removed – and that is all it took! The subtle adjustment of decision thresholds and introduction of delays broke the cycle and a steady state was then restored.

Where is the energy?

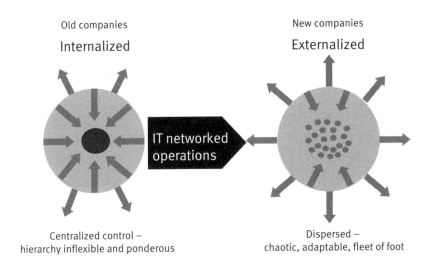

Old companies
Internalized

New companies
Externalized

IT networked operations

Centralized control –
hierarchy inflexible and ponderous

Dispersed –
chaotic, adaptable, fleet of foot

Companies are moving to more adaptive and adaptable modes

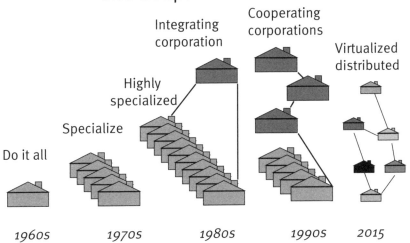

Integrating corporation

Cooperating corporations

Virtualized distributed

Highly specialized

Specialize

Do it all

1960s   1970s   1980s   1990s   2015

Inside companies and organizations the product of rapid market and technology change is often an apparent chaos that can be detected when:

$$\textit{Mean Time Between Decisions} >> \textit{Mean Time Between Surprises}$$
$$\text{and}$$
$$\textit{Mean Time Between Managers} >> \textit{Mean Time Between Reorganizations}$$

It is also a fundamental indication of the inability to respond to change usually associated with old minds, thinking, structure and modes of operations. Unfortunately the final outcome is not pretty – companies can dissipate all their resources and energy and reorganize themselves into liquidation!

If we take the dot-com bust for a moment and list the causes of collapse, we get:

- human greed
- the lemming effect, where we expect one success to herald another
- a belief that old market and business principles could be abandoned
- a mantra that said profit really did not matter
- the old economy conspiring to protect itself, and biting back

Not many people would cite the lack of bandwidth in our networks or the lack of management ability to adapt to IT and away from paper as also being root causes. It is equally unlikely that anyone would probably identify governments as having any responsibility. Yet their action in driving up the price of 3G mobile network licences to an absurd level actually precipitated a huge crash of the telecommunications industry across Europe and the rest of the world. All of which added to the avalanche of negative market confidence.

This really was a case of people looking at a limited number of parameters, making an assessment on that basis and deciding to do something that was fundamentally stupid. Only this time our speed of networking ensured that they all did the same thing at almost the same time across multiple aspects of the IT and telecom sector.

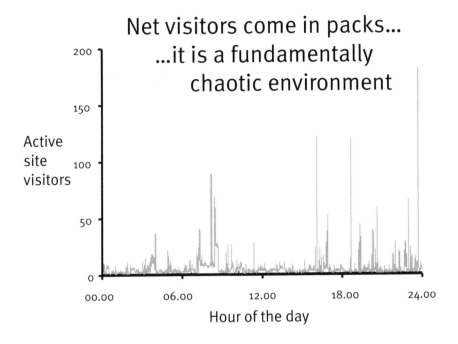

Net visitors come in packs...
...it is a fundamentally chaotic environment

Active site visitors

Hour of the day

Byte 15
Short-Term Economics

As I watch the actions of companies and governments it often seems that our species has lost the ability for joined-up thinking and economics.

Have giant corporations and governments thrown away 60 IQ points along with the ability to make rational decisions beyond simple-minded upfront or face-value costings? All companies and organizations face difficult choices and crisis conditions that sometimes lead to limited options and odd decisions. Large and small, they all make errors and suffer the mistakes of others outside their control. But there is no excuse, and no place, for short-term stupidity and muddled thinking that damages the long-term operation and viability of any group, company or country.

At home, individuals think long term and paint the house instead of letting it rot, service the car rather than risk an accident, pay for children's education rather than rendering them unemployable in later life. But what do these same people do at work? Hold back on investment to secure short-term gain or favour, to secure their position and that of their team, and all at the expense of the future. They will neglect building, infrastructure, services and people training, focus on the trivial and generally screw up. How come?

All healthcare systems are reeling under increasing demand and pressure from ageing populations that expect to live forever, and implant technologies have become a big deal. In a recent report on chip implants for Parkinson's and related diseases it was argued that the $30k per patient necessary to affect individual repairs was too expensive. So every year thousands are rendered virtually useless to society, condemned to an undignified end, at a massive cost to their families, friends, companies and nation. Apart from humanitarian considerations, each patient will dissipate at least $100k of resource between disease onset and death. Add to this the lost productivity through an inability to work, the cost of continued sibling support and distraction etc., and it is obvious that the economics of denial make no sense in the long term. This is all made even more incongruous by rapidly ageing populations that need more care, and the year-on-year falling numbers of potential carers, whilst the allocation funds to support those with self-inflicted injuries and diseases through drug abuse, alcohol and tobacco is being ramped up out of all proportion. Here there is little or no chance of any social or financial payback and even less chance of a technological solution. The entire decision base is generally humanitarian, emotional and social rather than economic. But it is the same body making the decision!

The media coverage of anthrax in the USA, and CJD in the UK, or SARS in the Far East, would have us believe that we face problems of epidemic proportion and $Ms have been spent trying to contain such potential threats. But on a global scale these are relative non-events with only hundreds of lives in danger compared to over 100,000 certain deaths each year attributed to influenza, and the 3000 a day due to malaria. At the other end of the spectrum, many hospitals seem to have forgotten the basic hygiene lessons of Lister in 1865 and decided that money can be saved on cleaning contracts. So, dirty hospitals claim the lives of hundreds of people/week, prematurely dispatched by MRSA and other infections. Along with this, our war chest of antibiotics continues to be depleted by overuse and abuse.

People continue to be tragically killed in unnecessary railway accidents. Did somebody decide not to invest in safety checks, new tracks, signalling equipment and rolling stock in order to save on the operating costs? In some cases the net result of such deaths is $Bns lost in national productivity and commuter time, and track repairs far exceeding the original savings. How strange that we kill tens of thousands per year in road accidents and fail to invest more than petty cash on the repair, maintenance and expansion of the basic road infrastructure. They say speed kills, but mostly it seems to be bad roads. So, will we see government officers charged with the equivalent of corporate manslaughter? I think not!

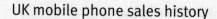

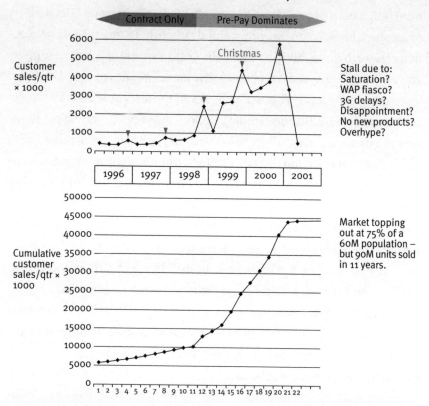

The dot-com boom and bust, and the stalling of the economy, has largely been brought about by a basic lack of bandwidth. Yet the recent 3G mobile license fiasco saw the EU telecoms industry raped of over $100Bn. If only $50Bn of that money had been made available then every EU home and office could now be enjoying optical fibre bandwidth that would transform economies.

Silicon Valley and much of California have in recent times been zoned for power cuts due to the deregulation of the power industry and the non-cost effective activity of peak loading displaced by corporate greed. The Enron and WorldCom debacles implicated, and in some cases, brought down other big names in the consulting and financial sector. Was this entirely down to executive and corporate graft, or was it largely ignorance and blindness, coupled with a complete focus on the short-term gain? The list goes on!

Who is to blame for all this? How did we become so blind and dumb? I suspect it is down to complexity and dispersed responsibility. We have deployed technology that speeds up our communication and ability to enact decisions, but without simultaneously investing in models and aids to visualize and understand the outcome. In short, we have just not invested in the appropriate management tools and systems. It is not that appropriate models and tools don't exist, but more that we have not understood or valued the technology potential or the rate of change. The way we are running modern government and business is almost like trying to fly a jumbo jet with no instrumentation and the blinds down. But, as we are demonstrating by the week, Dickensian thinking will not work in a world of Star Trek communication and technology. We really do need a management upgrade!

Byte 16
No Market Savvy

You know the world is going crazy when the best rapper is a white guy, the best golfer is a black guy, the Swiss hold the America's Cup, France is accusing the US of arrogance and Germany doesn't want to go to war.

Unknown source

Control is out and chaos is in!

From the experience of the past two years I think we can safely say that no individual, company, institution or government understands the stock market. Experts are at last acknowledging that chaos is the dominant mode and all talk of control has at best been nonsense, at worst, hubris. Despite recent experience I still see published reports that proclaim that there is no new economy, dot-com is dead, and high tech was just some ghastly mistake. What a contrast to the market hysteria, greed and panic not to miss the boat of only a few months ago.

Those who by chance got in early, rode the eWave and jumped at the right time, laughed all the way to the bank, and those who didn't were left holding the baby and nursing their losses. Some of the dot-com boomers saw their net worth rise rapidly into the $100Ms only to fall to near zero in a matter of weeks. At some point it seemed everyone was a paper millionaire! So what went wrong? Was it all a mistake and will it all recover? Certainly when you look at the rise in dot-com spending with online retail and music (legal and illegal) sales, plus the buoyancy of the online travel market, it appears that dot-com is not only alive and well, it is booming.

When we look at the high-tech sector we need to consider the historical context. There have always been peeks and troughs, periodic shakeouts, growth followed by collapse; it is as natural as life itself. As new markets are created, set-

82

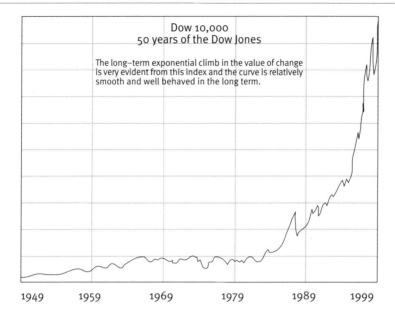

Dow 10,000
50 years of the Dow Jones

The long–term exponential climb in the value of change is very evident from this index and the curve is relatively smooth and well behaved in the long term.

1949   1959   1969   1979   1989   1999

tle down, and attain some reasonable growth they do so at the expense of the old, which diminish and die. For example, in 1900 there were over a thousand automobile manufacturers in the USA, but by 1930 this number was reduced to just four, producing far more vehicles than the original thousand.

Markets are fundamentally fickle and chaotic. Small changes can have a big impact, especially when the investor base has little loyalty and is subject to a mass herding mentality. Once a critical number of investment changes are made everyone follows the trend, no one wants to miss out, no one wants to be left behind. This is the power of fear, greed and short-termism.

At the most fundamental level, without a high-tech sector there is no industry, food, heat, light, power, waste disposal, water, medicine or indeed life. We are just as reliant on technological progress as we are on food. Those countries that feel that they can develop an economy on a service industry alone with absolutely no hardware industry may be sitting on a time bomb of brittleness in a world that is yet to achieve 100% peace and political stability.

It is all about speed of technology, creation and adoption, coupled with market adaptation and developments changing faster than human rationale. Evolutionary forces dominate all change, technological and biological. If we do nothing it will all ultimately come right, but the process will not be compassionate or comfortable. Evolution cares nothing for pain and suffering, she rolls the dice and accumulates the outcomes. Who survives or dies is of no direct interest to evolution as the adaptable and fleet of foot gain over the strong and intellectual. Evolution is a mere spectator in the final outcome.

The reality is that the dot-coms caught a cold first, followed by the not dot-coms. Now we see overstretched companies and sectors beginning to fall, and even the venture capitalists are biting the dust. At a fundamental level, individuals and groups have invested money and time in the creation of far more companies than the global economy can support, and the excess are going to go to the wall. Some have become household names in months and gained the confidence and respect of millions, some hardly got off the starting line and a few have become a social necessity and will not die.

In many respects the global economy has never been so robust and vibrant. Inflation is on the ropes and unemployment relatively low, whilst the creation of new companies has become more measured. There may be cause for gloom and despondency on one level, but in terms of globalization, I think we can be reasonably optimistic in the long term.

All transitions engender some difficulties, stresses and strains upon society. It is unfortunate that our technology creates change faster than we can anticipate and adapt. Therein lies an opportunity for us to model situations before we embark on the wholesale deployment of the new. I fear our ability to understand and comprehend in time will always be limited. By its very nature, technology does radical things, and we only have to look at the dot-com revolution to see how very different it is and how it affects everyone on the planet. The production or movement of atoms does not impose a limit on this new economy, as it deals with the infinite world of networked bits.

It seems that the old economy was determined to slow down the dot-com world and tried to negate the progress as it was created, but in reality it is being dragged along and will have to change. Over 91% of UK businesses use the Internet and over 80% place orders online, and <1% worry about security and privacy. Those that don't fully understand and grasp the change will see the basics of the old economy disrupted by new business models and modes. Much of what we have done in the past is ecologically unsustainable, but new technologies offer solutions and a different route to sustainable lifestyles. I think we'll just have to wait and see, but not for long, as control is out and chaos is in!

Byte 17
How Was Christmas Online For You?

Is e-tail about to put real world shopping to shame, with far reach-ing consequences?

Christmas 2002 was a watershed in my consumer life. It was the year when I purchased more gifts and spent far more money online than in physical stores. I suspect I am not alone in this because the UK saw its first £1Bn of online sales in one month, while the US saw the first $1Bn of online sales in a single week.

With over 45% of households online in both countries it looks like Joe Public have overcome their Internet security fears and taken the plunge into the e-world. According to the latest figures, 1.3% of all US retail purchases are now made online, and in the UK this figure is 4%. When you consider the shopping experience, the relative inconvenience and service levels of the two countries, I can easily understand why. The positive selling attitude, modern mall facilities, parking and road transport of the US makes physical shopping a pleasure, while the converse is the case in the UK and much of the EU. Poor facilities, poor infrastructure, high prices, and nowhere to park your car are major retail impediments.

I have been making online purchases from the very outset of the com-mercial Internet and I have seen online shops progress from the truly awful to the truly brilliant. What I really like is the availability of goods and serv-ices, the high-quality service, the price and delivery – all invariably better than any offline alternative.

This year the situation was amplified by my efforts to simultaneously buy a computer, a digital camera, two 120MByte hard drives, and sundries from a well-known high street chain. I had all the items I wished to purchase

Reasons for shopping online

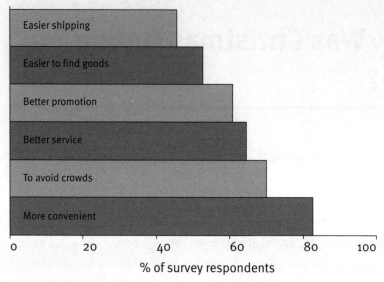

Easier shipping	
Easier to find goods	
Better promotion	
Better service	
To avoid crowds	
More convenient	

% of survey respondents

Source: Vivendi 2001

EU online best buys

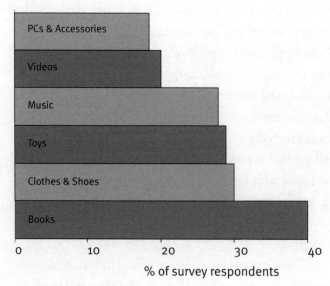

PCs & Accessories	
Videos	
Music	
Toys	
Clothes & Shoes	
Books	

% of survey respondents

Source: Juniper Medici Metrix 2001

in front of me but I was told I could not buy the computer. How come? It turned out that the chosen computer was the last of the line and the display model was the only one left. No matter what I said, the manager would not let it go. This was to be a cash transaction – a pick-it-up-and-take-it-away-right-now purchase, a no-hassle deal – but it didn't matter. The manager was quite positive – in a negative direction, ('We can order one for you sir, yada, yada …') – but he didn't really want to help me.

My wife will be the first to say I was not on the front row when patience was handed out, and I suddenly felt myself snap. If I can't have the computer then I really don't want this camera with the extra memory card, the two 120MB hard drives, and other sundries, no matter what. I walked out of the store having purchased nothing. The staff member involved got all panicky as I headed to the door, but the manager actually let a £2000-plus sale slip through his hands. It all beggared belief – well, my belief anyway.

The next day I eventually found the computer I was looking for in another store and I made a purchase without incident. However, they didn't have the camera or hard drives I needed. These were ordered online at around 15:00 hours on that day – 23 December. I received confirmation of the order within minutes by email and a confirmation of shipping at around 17:00 the same day. To my amazement, the entire order arrived intact by 13:00 on 24 December. This was phenomenal, no-nonsense, customer-centred service. It was far cheaper too!

So far I have purchased flowers, books, toys, tools, CDs, DVDs, computer hardware and software, plus an assortment of services online. On every occasion I have been well served and pleased with the outcome. To date my credit card number and details have only been hijacked twice, but on both occasions that was via conventional retail transactions and not the Internet. For me, security has never been an issue in the sense that the Internet has never posed anything remotely like the risk presented by the old world of coin, paper, cheque and card.

Being in the midst of the dot-com revolution I can confirm the eWorld has not gone away or slowed down, despite being unfashionable. It has just continually and quietly expanded since the much publicized and overstated dot-com bust.

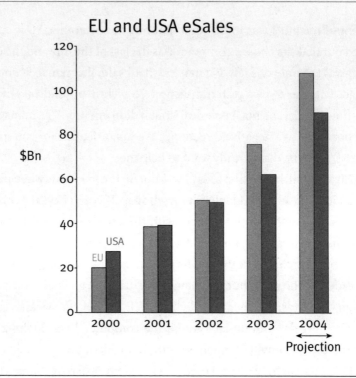

Have a nice day

A wonderful and astute observation on the shopping experience in two differing cultures by an American friend now living in the UK: 'I would sooner be told to *have a nice* day by someone who doesn't mean it, than told to *f*** off* by someone that does.'

A slightly different interpretation was furnished by another American friend who observed that: 'Shop assistants in the USA are so much nicer and friendlier than in the UK because they are never sure if the customer is carrying a gun or not!'

While the UK is around eighth place in the broadband league be-hind Korea, Singapore, Japan, Scandinavia, the US, Canada and Germany, around 45% of UK households are online, and huge numbers of people with Internet access in their offices. So, strangely, the UK seems to be developing a bit of a lead in terms of online sales.

Against all the odds, UK business has also established a lead in terms of business-to-business transaction rates that are ahead of the USA per capita. Could it just be that the adversity of poor service and infrastructure is biting back in the form of the online alternatives? For me the answer has to be 'yes', and my guess is that 90% of my Christmas 2003 purchases will be online, while that of the UK will exceed 10%.

When we started the dot-com boom the gurus said it would change everything. They were right but probably more right than even they could have guessed.

Byte 18

Wrong Shopping Protocol

Visit a physical store, check out the goods, and then purchase on-line.

My wife and daughters will tell you that I really don't like shopping. A typical man they say, as after about the first hour I start to scan for the first coffee shop I can find. Of course there are far too few technology stores, in which I can easily lose an hour, and the prospect of a clothing-only focus tends to clinch the day. It isn't the dread of spending money, but the sheer amount of time expended and the Dickensian processes involved that seem to get to me. I am definitely a hunter and not a gatherer!

Every time I go into a modern store, search for the goods I need, make a decision, and get to the point of a sale, they ask me the same long string of questions they asked on all my previous visit. Name? Address? Telephone number? Postal code? Would you like an extended warranty? And so on. With my name this tends to be a protracted process along the lines – is that C-o-c-r? C-o-c-k? Oh, C-o-c-h-r-a-n, oh? Aha, with an 'e'?

After far too many of these encounters, I have taken to asking the individual sales people for control of the keyboard and screen. It usually evokes a look of surprise on their part, but it significantly reduces my frustration level and wastes a lot less time. It seems extraordinary that anyone would design a system that extracts the information in my brain by speech to someone else through their ears and then to the keyboard down their arms and fingers, when I am perfectly capable of typing the information myself. Even worse, why can't they just get all of the information off my credit card, loyalty card, mobile phone, or some other device? After all, on a PC you don't keep filling forms in, you do it once and then get the machine to do it for you thereafter.

It might seem trivial, but just watch the amount of time wasted at cash registers when buying something reasonably insignificant. Most machines are now linked to inventory and logistics control systems in order to streamline the back-end processes, but at the expense of the front end – you and me. On many occasions the customer and staff time wasted is worth far more than the item purchased and makes a hidden contribution to the recognized 47% of the global GDP that is transaction costs. It may be cost effective for the store to make us stand in line and wait for the attention of an overloaded sales person, and a poorly designed electronic point of sale protocol, but when you are in a hurry this is very frustrating.

It has been established that the length of the checkout line/queue modulates our purchases when we first enter a store. Long lines mean we buy less. Short lines mean we buy more. In both cases the amounts can span 5–15% which, for the store, can in the worst case be translated into a 10–30% loss. I, for one, will not join a queue (or line) of more than two to three people, and more especially if there is a problem that is about to extend the experience. The takings of any store are now limited by the checkout response time. Roll on the day when bar codes are replaced by RFID tags. Customers will be able to take control of the checkout process and become the masters of their own shopping destiny!

We could all benefit from a customer interface at every point of sale that affords us control, where we enter all the data and make the decisions. My name, address, postal code, date of birth, bank details and preferences regarding extended warranty, and anything else related to the purchase of goods, has remained static for years and unlikely to be updated in any significant way in the near future. As Spike Milligan wryly observed, you can't update your date of birth!

Wouldn't it be nice if stores, gas and railway stations developed memories so that we are recognized as we enter, our information is available at the point of sale, and the financial transaction becomes a minor part of the purchase process, as apposed to a major trauma at the end of a long day. If only I could enter hotels, airports and restaurants to be recognized and have my data available. I would like to stop carrying passports, driving licence, medical records and other data in paper or plastic form when they can be

Buying a PC on the High Street

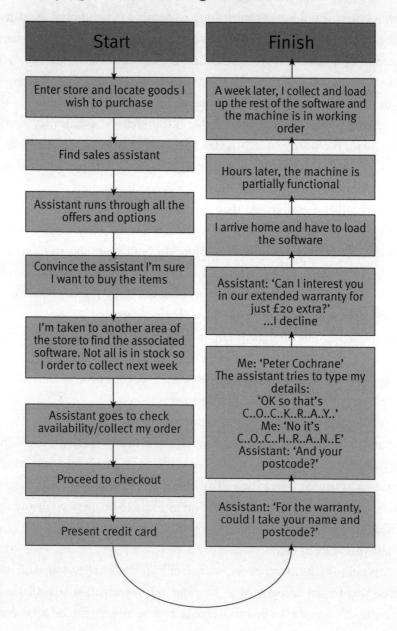

Buying a PC online

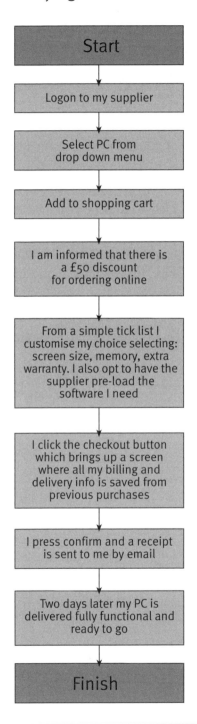

easily integrated onto a single device, but most of all I would like to stop answering the same string of questions each time I encounter a cash register or service desk.

Just give me a keyboard and a screen and I will type in all the relevant data for my commercial and leisure life once, and I will keep it updated – after all it is in my interest to have it correct and it is in my interest to present the right credentials. Just imagine how many data entry mistakes are made through verbal misunderstandings, and how much human life is wasted as a result. This is one aspect that I like about online shopping. Open an account and thereafter you are all set. I recently found myself migrating to a new and more productive protocol. Visit the physical store to check out the goods, and then return home to purchase online.

Today is a Saturday and another frantic shopping experience. My wife is deep into the experience. I had wanted to make a few purchases in this store, but the line is long, so it can wait, and the coffee smells great. For reasons I needn't explain here, I have my laptop with me and so I just accessed the Web site of the store and made my purchases online instead!

Byte 19
Chips in Everything – Including Me

A future of electronic tags and intelligence in everything from our grocery packaging to our clothes and bodies raises big questions about privacy and security.

Almost everything we now buy, including hardware, clothing and most foodstuffs, have a visible bar code used as the primary means of identification at points of sale. Everything is universally swiped. The digital ID goes into a cash register to be recorded, totalled and printed on a receipt. Unseen to us, the data often enters a stock control and logistics chain to keep the shelves stacked and supply flowing. The transition to this digital form has been rapid, almost invisible, and non-threatening.

The next phase already has some manufacturers embedding RFID (Radio Frequency IDentification) tags in their goods. For example, some trainers have them embedded in their soles, and some razors in their handles. What is an RFID tag? In this case, it is a small radio transceiver that is inert until energized by a radio beam of a given frequency. As a customer gets to a checkout, the beam energizes both receiver and transmitter components, and product information is sent to the register.

There are many reasons manufacturers and retailers welcome this technology. It allows much greater storage of information about a product's life than a bar code. Details about raw materials, transport, processing, assembly, delivery and sale can be captured. It also offers a higher degree of brand protection and authentication.

This technology establishes new and invaluable production control and audit trail systems, with substantial benefits expected in terms of quality control and production cost reduction. In the case of foodstuffs and con-

Why RFID?

- Production control and tracking
- Inventory and quality control
- *Brand protection*
- Ownership and security
- Logistics and pricing
- Electronic point of sale
- Customer relationship management (CRM)
- Customer support and service history
- Defence and tracking

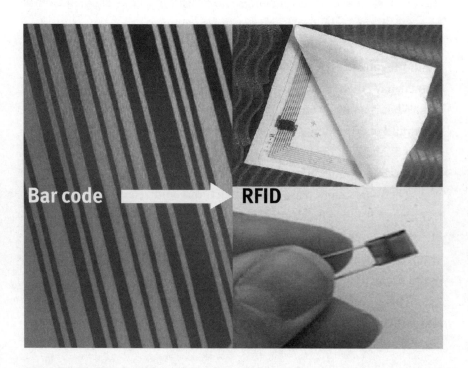

Bar code ➡ RFID

sumables, rapid identification and remedial action can be taken in the event of any contamination or defects with minimal disruption and waste to the supply chain, sales outlet, and customers.

But while bar codes are passive, and mostly perceived as just a price tag, many people will see RFID tags as another electronic threat challenging our civil liberties. It wouldn't take much of a technological leap to be able to detect your trainers and presumably you, entering a store, restaurant or cinema, for example. We might even contemplate the significance of two or more pairs of trainers in the same location! Perhaps a race, an arranged meeting, or a coincidence?

Fast forward ten years and assume all bar codes have been replaced by embedded RFID tags. Also assume we have accepted them into our everyday lives in much the same way we did the bar code. There are then many new and powerful scenarios we can conjure up, some of which we will like and some we will not.

For example, I might purchase a new TV, take it home and plug it into a power outlet. When I switch it on it would look around my home and say hello to my washing machine, microwave, radio, hi-fi and PC. All of this appliance information is shared and held within that new TV. If during the night someone burgles my home and steals my new TV, takes it to their home and plugs it in, it will immediately look around the building and say: 'Oh no, wrong washing machine, microwave, radio, hi-fi, PC – I think I'd better contact Peter Cochrane and the police, I've been stolen.' Most of us, I think, would applaud such a facility.

Other everyday experiences could also be enhanced and made more secure. Imagine arriving at the airport to have our face, eye, hand, thumb and voice automatically recognized and verified by computer. Our possessions are also identified through their RFID tags. The old cardboard passport or plastic ID card would no longer be required and we wouldn't have to wait in line at check-in or security.

Whilst waiting to board the plane we may make a few purchases and then be scanned again as we board. The system again identifies us, and recognizes all our clothing and possessions, including laptop, mobile phone and PDA. The system also recognizes we have purchased a bottle of wine and few other goods that are completely safe. But as the aircraft gets ready to taxi and take off, the security system is checking through the records of all the passengers and discovers a cause for concern. There are four people in the aircraft – two in first class, one in the middle section and one right at the back – who have at no time declared they know each other. None of their documentation indicates they are with the same company or organization but through examination of all of the RFID tags and records they contain, it becomes clear all four people have mobile phones and items of clothing purchased on the same day, from the same stores, using the same credit card.

Alarm bells start to ring in the security minds and questions are posed. What is happening? This is not a precise replay of events of 9/11 but it's not so far removed. Pre-9/11 there was a lot of information that associated the players in the plot to commit those devastating atrocities. They might have been intercepted had the authorities had the power of electronic tagging and accurate analyses developed and to hand. RFID tags will hand us such a capability on a plate. The big question in everyone's mind is going to be: where does security start and finish and the violation of personal privacy and civil liberties become a problem?

I think we will have to give up some of our civil liberties and personal freedoms to ensure our collective freedom and safety in future. It is probably going to be a small price to pay if we avoid another 9/11 or anything remotely like it.

All of this is really about choice – and I have already volunteered my body for any surgically implanted technology that will improve my security and safety. To be identified instantly, to be tracked constantly and to have all my medical and other records available would need more than an RFID tag. But whatever. Just sign me up. Or more correctly – plug me in – track away and keep me safe!

Personally I feel relaxed about all of this provided it is only accessible to the right people, and any internal tagging remains a voluntary act on the part of the participant.

Byte 20
The Cyborgs Are Here

It is increasingly apparent that we are on course to becoming a part of our own technology.

Millions already carry sophisticated electronics embedded in their bodies. Pacemakers, artificial hearts, respiratory stimulators and pain relief modules are now installed in prolific numbers to sustain otherwise threatened lives. At the forefront of experimentation further developments have allowed paraplegics to control computers by thought, the sightless to see shadowy images for the first time, and spinally damaged patients have achieved a limited movement in otherwise disconnected limbs.

Small chip sensors and radio units implanted in the brain collect and transmit neural pulses to a computer, and the brain can adapt to move a mouse and select keys. An artificial retina implant has given very poor-resolution sight to a few previously unable to see. Robotic limbs have been connected directly to the human nervous system. But there is a long way to go before we achieve a Steve Austin. The scale of difference between where we are, and a fully engineered, patient adequate performance is on a par with the difference between a crystal set of the early 1900s and a modern PC. But our technological progress is now far faster than in 1900 and we may only have to wait another 20 years or so.

So, the part human–part machine is not far away. But the technology doesn't have to be ugly and threatening like the Borg in Star Trek – it can be beautiful and be used to repair and restore people to their former health. I have a vested interest in such technologies as I am becoming increasingly deaf, and my pancreas dysfunctional. To date my ears are 25dB and 15dB down, and my hearing range limited to frequencies below 9kHz. This is

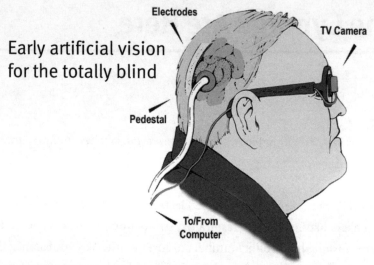

Early artificial vision for the totally blind

Electrodes

TV Camera

Pedestal

To/From Computer

Reproduced by kind permission of the Dobelle Group and Lipincott, Williams & Wilkins

Artificial vision for the totally blind – an early prototype system

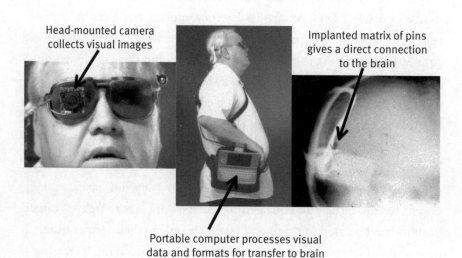

Head-mounted camera collects visual images

Implanted matrix of pins gives a direct connection to the brain

Portable computer processes visual data and formats for transfer to brain

Reproduced by kind permission of the Dobelle Group and Lipincott, Williams & Wilkins

about half of the normal range. As a result, conversations in noisy environments are increasingly difficult, and I tend to deafen others with the volume of TV and hi-fi. I suspect my weakening pancreas will soon see me resorting to insulin. This is all a growing and interesting experience, and whilst I often receive sympathy for my diabetes, not so for my growing deafness!

Of course my wish would be to have my physical shortcomings repaired and restored using the same materials of which I am constructed – carbon. I suspect that genetic engineering will get there sooner than expected, as artificial hearing elements such as cartilage for lobes, skin for drums, and linkages to the inner ear are already available. However, an artificial cochlea sub-assembly connected directly to the auditory nerve seems some way off.

In the short term I would happily subsume any form of electronic technology into my body to overcome my current, and any future, limitations. However, my inclination would be to also enhance my hearing well beyond the original specification of our species, and I would also include other facilities such as an implanted radio and mobile phone. I have experimented with highly sensitive hearing augmentation involving microphones, low-noise amplifiers, and ear inserts. It is interesting to discover what we are all missing! The breathing of someone across a room, birds singing 500m away, the brush of feet on carpet, and the rustle of clothing as people walk.

If I can enhance my hearing, then I immediately want to enhance my sight. To see into the infrared and ultraviolet, to be able to switch colour in or out for the advantage of contrast afforded by pure black and white, would be life and survival enhancing. It is in this area of visually augmenting hearing that I suspect we would gain most. For me, the worst feature of gradual deafness is a degraded spatial awareness, of which ambient noise plays an important part in our perception processing. It would be a significant advantage to have this presented visually on a head-up display, along with text messages and other awareness-enhancing features such as noise direction and intensity indicators.

Another interesting opportunity I could add to my super-human wish-list is a real-time speech-to-text display. Subtitles on every conversation, TV broadcast and movie would be a real boon. All the basic technology is available today, only it is far too slow and cumbersome to be worn and carried for real-time use. But in 20 years it should be easily possible.

Predicting the future has always been risky, but the increasing speed of technology development is making it progressively easier, especially as most of our past efforts turned out to be so pessimistic. The future just seems to arrive faster every year! I think we can confidently assume that healthcare, remote working, education, trading, news, entertainment and almost everything will be increasingly online. As we continue to wear more technology, and accept more implants, the progress will continue. If we can control our functions and devices through implants and thinking, then there is also a real chance we will be able to communicate by the same means.

By 2025 our computers will be over 1,000,000 times more powerful than today, and our relationship with technology will have been transformed far more than in the previous 100 years. In some respects a Borg-like society is inevitable, but it doesn't have to be black and threatening; it can be made rich and life enhancing!

I was prompted to write much of the above during an internal EU flight. I had just offered a young Swedish lady a chocolate from my in-flight dinner tray with the explanation that I was a Type 2 diabetic and could not eat it. She kindly accepted and explained she was Type 1 and could! Her hidden secret was an insulin pump that dispensed insulin on demand – in effect an artificial, if crude, pancreas. So I was actually sat next to a blond, blue-eyed cyborg, not at all like the Borg in the Star Trek version!

Byte 21
Web Realities

The online population is less likely to see pornography and security as a problem, and <3% express any concern.

The commercial Internet has only been visible since 1995 and mobile phones didn't appear until 1989. In just a decade the PC, Internet and mobile phone have become accepted and dominant business tools and modes of communication. With real data on the Internet and its contribution to society, and the benefit of hindsight, all the past media debates, arguments and objections now seem quaint and a total waste of time. They also mirror previous debates about typewriters, telegrams, recorded music, radio and TV.

Recent studies show a surge in online sales and the abandonment of security fears regarding the use of credit cards. People have realized that the Internet is one of the safest forms of financial communication. It has also been discovered that the Internet is not dominated by a bunch of nerds in their bedrooms, but by educated and professional people with a higher than average disposable income. Men and women seem to spend almost the same amount of time on the Internet, but women focus on academic pursuits and their jobs, whilst men look to entertainment, commerce, games, music, purchasing and banking.

Surprisingly the young do not dominate the Internet; the age distribution is actually bimodal, with a suck-out of around about 35–40 years. Young and old seem to be on the Web in roughly equal numbers, and the middle group tend to be disadvantaged by work and the need to earn to support both!

Internet users as % of population(2001)

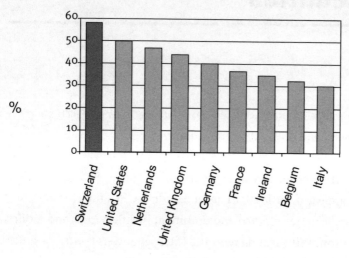

Source: http://www.geneva.ch/PPP.htm

The Internet veterans predominately gain access for news, trading and stocks, and have a work focus. Newcomers tend to focus on hobbies, music and entertainment. It appears that the majority of the non-Internet population want to get online and feel that they are being left behind. The population ratio of most to least avid users is ~4, and screen time (TV + PC) is almost a constant, with the PC gradually displacing TV.

In complete contrast to the fears of many, those who use the Internet actually read more books and newspapers, listen to more music and radio, and make most phone calls. Children exposed to PCs from the age of 3 upwards appear to gain about 20 IQ points by the time they are 15. In short, they become smarter rather than dumber as the pundits predicted. Engaging in computer games seems to engender a higher level of strategic thinking and adaptability, perhaps even making children more compatible with a world that is fundamentally chaotic.

In the USA over 40% of all homes have a computer; in much of Europe the percentage is even higher, and across most of the Western world, 60% of people have access to computers and the Internet at their workplace.

One big surprise that emerges from the online population is that they are less likely to see pornography and security as a problem. Less than 3% of the online population express any concern. Parents on the other hand feel that they have to police their children's PC and TV time and, specifically, the subject matter. But the children don't agree and get to do and see what they want anyway by bypassing their parents and their wishes.

Over 80% believe that they spend about the right amount of time online, and have not given up any of their non-screen activities such as sport, socializing and hobbies. They believe their lives have become more productive because they have gained from the computer and even more from the abandonment of TV. Internet users are far more optimistic about the advantages of IT technology than non-users.

Those people not yet online record scores that are more or less an inversion of all of the above. Of those that have declared no interest in the Internet, ~16% say they would never buy a computer or go online at any price. Overall it seems that 84% of those online have email accounts with over 40% checking their email more than once a day. Most have an 80% satisfaction level with the Internet; speed of access remains the key dissatisfaction parameter, and lack of broadband connectivity a major problem.

There now seems to be a new positive breed of anecdotes contributing to Internet growth. Looking back we can trace similar progress with the steam engine, automobile, telephone, radio and TV. I can remember TV debates about the bad influence of television programmes depicting nudity, violence, pop music, and using unacceptable language. Today it all seems so tame and society doesn't seem to have suffered for it. Perhaps what we are learning is that freedom actually works.

Out of all of this there seems to be a single useful constant – ten years. Over our recent technological progress during and since the Industrial Revolution, it always seems to take about ten years for society to accept the new. Cheque books, credit cards, standing orders, direct debit, Internet payments, computers in the home, mobile phones, digital cameras, VHS, CD, DVD etc. all took about ten years to be accepted and established.

At every societal and technological transition point the Luddite lobby has always mounted an energetic campaign to stop progress. It spawned the idea that typewriters would leave us with people unable to use a pen, television would turn everybody into zombies, computers would wreck education, pornography on VHS would corrupt the population etc. Of course there is a very small grain of truth in all of the objections, but the upside always proves to be far greater than the down.

The reality and great success of the Internet is that it has transformed the way we do business and become invisible in less than a decade. It is accepted everywhere as the business and societal norm, and proving highly beneficial. Only a few Luddites remain to be convinced, but they are now in the minority and fast becoming insignificant. Perhaps the useless and pointless debates will rapidly go away too.

Byte 22

Another Management Goof!

Why do managers who are overtly enthusiastic and proud of their children come to work so negative in respect to the people they employ?

Over the past 40 years I have witnessed many management revolutions that have involved cycles of centralization and decentralization, quality management, corporate reengineering, people empowerment and emergent economies. At the same time there have been a plethora of motivation programmes for individuals, teams and managers.

Most programmes were really about changing company direction and culture in concert with technology and market demands. The key principle drawn from all the experiences is that treating people with respect and responsibility sees them respond accordingly. Getting everyone to buy-in and get focused on the company and customers generally works – people really do want to see their company succeed and prosper.

It always seemed to me to be paradoxical that managers who were overtly enthusiastic and proud of their children came to work so negative in the prospect, promotion and encouragement of the people they employ. After all they were dealing with the children of others! When I was asked to give a series of management lectures on the techniques I employed to create successful groups, projects and products I broached this early in Lecture 1. To the consternation of the audience I asked if they had sons and daughters. For those who said yes, I asked if they would break the arms and legs of their children for being able to run and swim faster than their parents? After a few shocked looks I further explained that these same managers were metaphorically breaking the arms and legs of the company employees.

Three kinds of people

There are those who:

- Make things happen
- Watch things happen
- Wonder what happened

My people loyalty credo:

- My family
- My people
- My company
- My country
- The planet

All companies and organizations have more than a responsibility to their shareholders and the bottom line; they also have a responsibility to their employees and society in general. When people are within our management gift, we are responsible for their well-being in the broader context of the company and industry. We are sanctioned to promote the future of employees to the best of our ability, not to identify them as a potential competitor and threat, to be disabled at every opportunity.

Today, technology offers unparalleled opportunities for managers and mentors at all levels to get it badly wrong. The worse cases I have witnessed include working environments where people are monitored continuously in terms of their keyboard activity and time spent staring at a monitor. No attempt is made to assess effectiveness. This is crude, wasteful and ultimately demotivating for all concerned.

Organizations need to monitor and measure their effectiveness, to challenge working practices and modify operations in concert with technology, markets and customers. But this has to be realized in a positive and reinforcing manner, not by draconian and threatening mechanisms of dubi-

---

Nothing much has changed ...

'Nothing is more difficult than to introduce a new order. Because the innovator has for enemies all those who have done well under the old conditions and lukewarm defenders in those who may do well under the new.'

Niccolò Machiavelli, 1513 AD

---

ous worth. The workforce has to be carried and encouraged rather than be demotivated and demoralized.

If you wanted to get it badly wrong and create a warehouse full of problems it is difficult to imagine anything better than some of the techniques supported and sanctioned by governments. For example: how would you feel if all your snail mail had been opened and read, your email had been scrutinized, and every time you made a phone call you knew someone was listening? Your state of tension and suspicion would be heightened if conversation after conversation gave a glimmer that you were living in some pseudo-police state that monitored your every breath.

If the office gossip involved things that only you were supposed to know, your apprehension would quickly accelerate. To say the least it would be disconcerting and threatening, and you would immediately modify your habits – in short you would become defensive.

Amazingly, some companies in what we consider to be the free and civilized world have been given the statutory right to snoop on employees' phone calls, snail mail and email by their governments. I am no lawyer, but this all seems to me a contravention of the very basic human right to privacy. The people responsible for invoking such systems have demonstrated a monumental lack of management skill and understanding and, perhaps worse, they have broadcast a complete lack of human and technical savvy. What happened to all those workshops and management revolutions where people would be empowered and made responsible, with companies investing in employees?

One of my management heroes is General George C. Patten who had an interesting 'take that hill' style of telling people what to do, without telling them how to do it. As far as I can see the only people who might profit from snooping, in the broad sense, are lawyers. Sooner or later, someone will take

Managerial thinking and practice

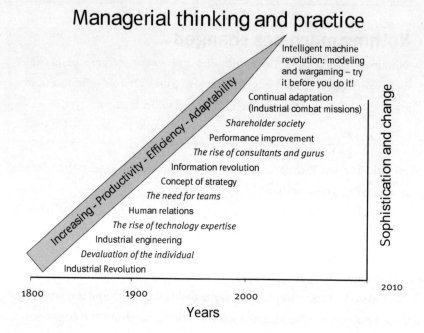

legal action and further slow down and cripple those engaged in the micro-management of individual thought and action.

For sure, inverse empowerment does not work – as ably demonstrated by every totalitarian and communist state, past and present. I suspect a lot of time and ingenuity has been devoted to sidelining the efforts of the snoopers who may be watching a virtual human typing on the keyboard, with a monitor viewed with less than 50% of the available attention span. What an opportunity for a non-management fight-back! One keystroke GOTO 3: take last weeks activity and LOOP; EXE Virtual Work ++++

Might it just be that a move back to the simplest form of monitoring might be timely and profitable? Instead of being obsessed by the email content and Internet activities of the individual, how about looking at the input and output, number of successful closures, and earnings per station. Further, let's compare the performance of individuals and groups, share the techniques to raise the bar for everyone, feeding back success as reward, create a few heroes and celebrate achievement. Probably a bit too basic and archaic I guess, after all this is only the 21st century – better get back to counting the pencils, paper clips, sheets of paper, attendance and coffee breaks ...

Byte 23
Porno or No Porno?

The human race has engaged in pornography for thousands of years, but we now have a vastly superior distribution network.

The last five years have seen thousands of arrests across the planet relating to child pornography, with the confiscation of obscene computer images. The most recent campaign hardly saw a day go by without some public figure being arrested. All are tracked down by their credit card details recovered from a few hard drives by the police across several nations. Many of those arrested deny the charges and you have to wonder at their stupidity in using their own credit card, their morals in wanting to participate in this awful trade, and the possibility that they may be innocent as a result of their card details being stolen. Only time and the courts will tell!

Historically, the human race has engaged in all forms of pornography and devious acts for thousands of years. In Elizabethan England, for example, young girls were often married at the age of 11 or 12 to much older men, and in ancient Rome, Egypt, Greece, China etc., the sexual practices and publications were at least the equal of those today. But we now have the technology to surpass any of the artistic rendering and static images of the ancients, and a vastly superior distribution network.

When photography first became commercially available a very old industry soon realized the potential and a new phase for pornography began. The ability to create high-quality images was suddenly available for widespread and rapid distribution. Soon, the dirty-mackintoshes and postcard sellers arrived, followed by the development of movies, TV, VHS, the PC, Internet, camcorders and digital cameras. Today the porn industry is ubiquitous, easily accessible, and at a price all can afford. It is a global industry

In 2002

- Users searched for *sex* more than games; travel; music; jokes; cars; weather; health; and jobs *combined*
- The top five search words in order = sex; mp3; hotmail; porno; pornography
- 36% of all Internet users visit adult sites – more than the total visiting online auction sites
- *80% of employees abuse Internet privileges – downloading porno/pirated software*
- 60% of employees visit Web sites or surf for personal use at work
- 70% of all Internet porn traffic occurs during the nine-to-five workday
- 17% of US firms have fired employees for misusing the Internet
- 26% of US firms have given workers formal reprimands and 20% have issued informal warnings
- 20% of men and ~12% of women admit to using their work computers to access sex sites
- *8M subscribers log on to porn sites every day and pay ~$100 for a year*

that overshadows Hollywood and rivals the production and supply of many manufactured goods. It is also that component of cable, satellite and hotel TV that makes them sell. In general everyone denies viewing, but the figures tell a different story. In some sense we are all guilty – depending on how pornography is defined! Books, newspapers, magazines, advertisements, TV, movies all contain pornography by someone's definition and standards.

Some years ago I was engaged in net-porn studies including availability, lack of national control, the meaningless nature of international borders, and legal ineffectiveness. The most important aspect was the all-too-apparent threat to children and the need for safe sites. At first, it was necessary to search for porn, and the content and access was crudely presented. But over the past decade the industry has become very sophisticated with the best-engineered sites and interfaces. You no longer have to try hard to find good-quality porn, it tends to find you! And once you have clicked, the systems can lock you in and web browser images appear rapidly, and often uncontrollably, on your screen. Not surprisingly, the dominant searches on the Web rapidly became sex related, only to be overtaken (it is rumoured) by MP3 and medical enquires in recent months.

As I travel the planet I occasionally scan the adult Pay TV channels in hotels and homes and, from time to time, search the Web. As far as I can see there is almost everything imaginable for free, and mostly harmless, in the strict sense, to normal adults. The content is vast in breadth and depth, with a wide range of depravities you wish you hadn't seen. I once recall watching a TV programme about landmines and what they do to people, and I wish I hadn't seen that either. In fact that programme and subject seemed to embody more obscenity than any porn site. But, in both cases I think we have to see a sample, to get the idea, to understand what is out there, what is good, bad and evil. We then have to decide on an appropriate course of action – what technology can provide, it can also take away!

Should we be worried about all this, or should we just ignore it, and continue to liberalize and relax our laws and policing, or should we try and clamp down? In reality, there is little or no chance of invoking any effective control. So what of those evil people who seek to involve children and other innocent or coherced groups? The immediate reaction of most people is to say we must stop them and apply absolutely draconian controls. However, like much of our new eConomy, I suspect we should do the opposite. We should encourage these individuals and groups to expose themselves (excuse the pun) on the Web; we can then gather and record their details, find out where and who they are. They are never going to go away, and legislation will only drive them underground, making it very difficult to track them down, and allowing them to become an even bigger danger.

Rather than panic at the rising tide of porno, and despite the fact that years ago someone tried to abduct one of my children, I think we should relax and draw a line that society deems to be acceptable. Our limited resources should then be focused on those dedicated to harming the young, innocent and defenseless. The really good news is that we can do this at very low cost, and very effectively over the Web. A really wise move would be to invest in the development of all technologies that can be used to guard and protect our children, and moreover, make it freely available and easy to self-install and use.

We should also try to keep a real perspective and remember that the upside of the Web is massive compared to the pornographic downside. Paper images, letters, photographs and movies via the postal system are a really uncontrollable proposition. This is a global activity that can be more easily controlled by the net, on the net. And what next? Look out for the 2.5 and 3G mobile phones with full-colour screens and integral cameras. Yes, porno is coming to a screen even closer to you!

Byte 24
Uncontrollable Bits

Transporting undesirable material across borders has become easier – despite post 9/11 crackdowns.

Just 20 years ago I was roaming the planet with a briefcase full of paper and 35mm slides. The order of the day was pre-packed carousels and VHS tapes, all ready for presentation at conferences and customers seminars – that is, if you wanted to be on the cutting edge of technology. Security and content control were not an issue for my company, most organizations or indeed me. It was an all-so-simple and straightforward world of locked cases and filing cabinets. Unfortunately, on one occasion I came close to falling foul of the control mechanisms of an individual political regime that I had not even contemplated, let alone considered.

I unwittingly came very close to being the victim of a local legal system as I entered a country for the first time. At the border crossing I simply walked in carrying my slides and videos, unquestioned and unimpeded, no problem! At the conference I loaded up my materials as usual, gave my presentations and was rewarded by a string of congratulatory comments that culminated in the chilling words: 'How did you get those videos into the country so fast?'

I responded to this strange situation with a confused: 'What do you mean?' The reply: 'Didn't you know that there is a strict control of all video material in this country and it has to be viewed and certified suitable for public viewing?' I felt the colour drain from my face, my heart rate increase and my skin go clammy. This was a police state, a place where freedom had yet to arrive. I had just walked in carrying potentially illegal materials and never given it a second thought.

I suddenly realized I had broken the local laws, committed a crime and was potentially subject to some heinous punishment. Further enquiry revealed that getting videos into this particular country could take up to six months and I had circumvented the whole process by blindly walking through customs, looking very innocent and truthfully stating that I had nothing to declare.

What to do? On the spot I decided I would donate all my videos to the conference organizers. There was no way I was going to attempt to exit the country carrying them, especially as I would find it extremely difficult not to look guilty as I did so. A few days later I departed with a half-empty briefcase. I had my carousels of 35mm slides but no videos.

That time now seems long gone and I can recall the incident with mild amusement. I was very lucky. In subsequent years I saw people who were not so fortunate, and it highlighted to me that ignorance is no defence in the eyes of the law, even when you are travelling to a country whose customs and laws you are not acquainted with.

For the rest of that 35mm-, OHP- and VHS-carrying era I was sure to check on the local laws and conditions of every country I visited. In the West we have become so accustomed to freedom that we take it for granted. You cannot make the same assumptions for all parts of the world.

Today we have migrated from hardware to software. All my presentation material, which includes slides, photographs, movies, animations and much more, is now stored on my laptop. As a result I can travel freely from one country to another and at no time does anyone ask: 'What are you carrying?', 'What material do you have?' 'Have you got any movies?' The controls are still there for VHS, CD and DVD, but not laptops.

Since 9/11 and the subsequent tightening of security across the planet, I have had cause to reflect on the state of play of data transportation and the lack of security. Almost everything we now buy has processing power and embedded memory. For example, my digital camera contains a 350MB hard drive onto which I can load any form of data. Using modest encryption software I could scramble, change format, embed and hide any kind of file on my camera, mobile phone, PDA and even my key ring. Walking into a

The old marketplace...
...*the customer view...*

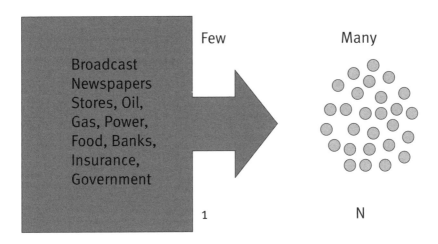

The Internet marketplace...
...*customer view...*

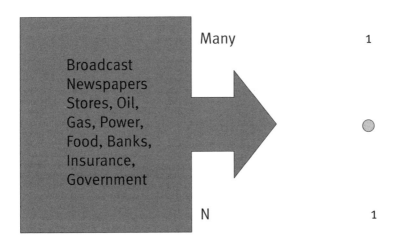

country unchecked and unimpeded is getting easier. And I suspect that the number of human couriers entering police and controlist states is growing

Along with the vast majority of humanity I do not have an evil disposition, want to cause mayhem, break the law or do anything wrong. I do not carry, communicate or transport information that would be of advantage to any dubious organization or the criminal and terrorist fraternity. What I do carry is commercial information – concepts, ideas and memos that I hope will result in progress. But my email account contains over 30,000 individual messages, and the number of other documents I carry is far in excess of this. So in some respects I enjoy the security of numbers – finding anything of interest or use can be difficult!

What has become clear is just how easy it is to turn advantageous technology around to some pernicious cause. I see no solution to the policing of data transportation across country boarders or continents. Each of us can now carry huge libraries of data on our hard drives and DVDs, encrypted and/or disguised to look innocent or otherwise. Faster screening of such databases at this time would appear impossible and futile in a world that is becoming totally connected.

Without some uniformity of laws and customs across the planet I see the number of innocent and intended transgressions accelerating with bit flow, increasing our individual risk. The good news is that most people will be unaware, and the chances of being detected are extremely low, and in the vast majority of cases no harm will be done.

Byte 25
Who Goes There?

*What lengths would you go to feel safe or to avoid being hassled at
security checks regularly? How about managing both these things?*

In the past 25 years I have crossed the Atlantic hundreds of times and I have
never been tempted to hijack an aircraft or take hostages. But it now seems
the system has to assume that I am a potential terrorist. On every single
flight from now on it seems I will have to prove I have no evil intent. I wasn't
a terrorist on the last 100 flights and, funnily enough, I'm still not a terrorist
on this one!

It is another early Sunday morning at Heathrow Terminal 4, and in my
check-in line are a lot of high-net-worth individuals trying to traverse the
planet, do business and create wealth. Every step of the way they are dogged
by 19th-century security systems. Don't get me wrong, I'm not against
security. I'm all for it, but I just watched an elderly lady have her handbag
searched and the security personnel removed a nail file, a pair of tweezers
and a pair of scissors. The gentleman immediately in front of me had his
safety razor confiscated. I just could not resist commenting that it would be
a pretty slow death – to be taken down a sliver at a time by a safety razor.

Since 9/11 I have progressively trimmed down my luggage to the point
where I know there is nothing that will trigger electronic scanners or attract
the attention of the X-ray operator. Even my trouser belt, wallet and zippers
have been selected so as not to set off alarms and engender all the hassle that
follows. I have just two bags, one containing my laptop and the other carrying no more than three days' clothing. My idea of travel is to never have
to check in a bag, never let go of any luggage and carry minimal clothing.
The probability of an airline losing your bag is between 1/100 and 1/1000,

Laws of security!

1   Deployment of resources is inversely proportional to actual risk

2   Perceived risk never = actual risk

3   Security people are never their own customers

4   Cracking systems is 100 × more fun than defending them

5   'Security standards' is an oxymoron

6   There is always a threat

7   The biggest threat is always in a direction you're not looking

8   You need two security departments – one to defend and one to attack

9   People expect 100% electronic security

10 Nothing is 100% secure

11 Security and operational requirements are mutually exclusive

12 Hackers are smarter than you – *they are younger!*

13 Legislation is always over five years behind the technology

14 As life becomes faster and chaotic it becomes less secure

15 *People are the number-1 risk factor. Machines are perverse, but they ain't devious – yet!*

and the chances of getting a cab, after your bag emerges last on the luggage belt, is zip! Better still, if your flight gets cancelled or changed, and you have checked your bag, you just lost a valuable degree of freedom in the equation of travel problem-solving!

The secret to lightweight travel is to make liberal use of hotel laundry and cleaning services rather than carry too much. For those difficult trips with nightly hops from one location to another, I use FedEx to dispatch clothes home and receive clean clothes in far-flung places. And so security has become the major factor in my efficiency equation.

I have just walked through unchallenged with pens and credit cards. All could easily make weapons for those of malicious intent. Moreover, once on the flight, I can purchase any number of potential weapons, a broken wine or whisky bottle, for example. During the in-flight meal, I am given a plastic knife and fork that are also potentially dangerous.

Is there something more intelligent that can be done to ensure the safety and speed of our passage? It seems to be a basic information problem. All the data about us is available somewhere, but unfortunately it isn't available at the airport. You would think a regular traveller would be accepted by security compared to the irregular passenger who suddenly turns up. We have the technology to recognize the human face, hands, fingers, body, voice, lips and various parts of the eye including the retina and iris.

Many years ago I volunteered to accept a chip implant that would replace my passport, credit card, and medical and membership cards to identify me immediately so I could pass through any form of security barrier unimpeded. At the time, all manner of objections appeared in the media but it now seems to be an imperative for those in a hurry. As a regular traveller I have found that the time taken to travel to and from airports, plus time to pass through security and immigration, now exceeds the time to fly from one continent to another.

In priority order, current technologies able to recognize people electronically are as follows:

- Implanted chips concealed inside the human body provide the highest level of security and information. This can include medical records, banking details and insurance, and travel details made available anywhere to those with an appropriate level of authority.
- Second is iris recognition, which is far superior to any genetic or biometric test.
- Unfortunately, the simplest, cheapest and most popular methods are the least accurate. Facial recognition, fingerprints, voice prints and lip prints all suffer from high rejection rates. There is a saving grace here that is very simple to realize. Voice recognition has an error rate of around 1 in 100, facial recognition is much higher at about 1 in 1000, while fingerprints are better still at about 1 in 100,000.

Personal identification security cost

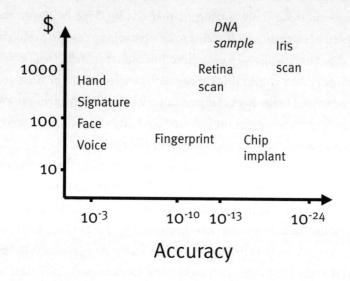

If we combine face, finger print and voice recognition, the error probability or rejection rate would then only be 1 in 10,000,000,000 for a cost of <$1000 per terminal. Iris scanners regularly achieve accuracy figures far in excess of 1 in 1,000,000,000,000,000,000,000,000 and are considerably better than DNA sampling.

So the technology to recognize people with great accuracy is available and so is the technology to identify known or likely terrorists. What is now required is a network capable of providing the necessary connectivity. In this new century, such a network will be essential to minimize the risk of external and internal attack.

As a regular traveller I would like to feel safe. Anyone can have any information about me and my organization to improve my security and safety, and that of others. I am still willing to volunteer for implanted chip technology that will allow me to walk into any airport anywhere and gain immediate access to the aircraft without having yet another body search.

Byte 26
Wireless Everything

Communicating wirelessly is attractive, for all kinds of reasons.

The past five years have seen an unusual transition in the number of wireless devices I own. I have the usual range of radios and televisions as well as VHS, DVD, tape and other disk recorders, but I have also installed or inherited a wireless-controlled garage door, security system, weather monitor, doorbell, intercom, and LAN. Of course, I also have mobile and cordless phones, walkie-talkies and numerous remote controls for toys and other pieces of IT including a myriad of infrared wireless devices. Suddenly, I am now in possession of more transmitters than receivers.

This change has mostly gone unnoticed as people use their key fob to unlock their car at a distance or use a remote for hi-fi and TV. What is really invisible is the radiation of energy across a broad range of frequencies. The planning and policing of radio is a complex task on a par with organizing air traffic systems. There have to be rules, regulation and control otherwise we would suffer wireless interference and very poor-quality service. Despite our best efforts this is sometimes experienced anyway – when atmospheric conditions cause unexpected interference, with signals propagating from one country to another in an unintended manner. The result is distorted TV pictures and poor audio reception.

Today, countries agree spectrum allocations (and channel frequencies) for broadcast, amateur and emergency services, remote control, military applications, cordless and mobile phones. But there are now devices and modes of operation that threaten this approach for the future. We have principally avoided interference by allocating specific frequencies of operations, separated in the same way that the different radio channels on your FM radio are allocated. With the arrival of far more short-range transmitters it is becoming increasingly difficult to avoid interference and the violation of agreed allocations. It is not unusual to install a wireless LAN (802.11 WiFi) and achieve 'right-first-time' operation. Sterling service over long periods is the norm, but short and unexplained periods of downtime are sometimes experienced. The usual culprit is an imported (and powerful) cordless phone creating interference across a wide area. It is extremely difficult to track down such devices, and they can cause a nuisance to everyone in the vicinity. In the defence of the purchaser it is not at all clear they are the culprit.

I see this situation getting worse as increasing numbers of wireless devices are produced. Just about every electrical and IT appliance radiates some energy and it is difficult to locate where interference originates. This is especially true if it involves correlating the activity of yourself, your children, spouse, neighbours and others, and what device they are using at a given time. And this is a problem that is going to accelerate with the arrival of Bluetooth and more strains of wireless LAN, as well as RFID tags, plastic cards etc., which will also contain transmitters in the near future. So it is imperative that we start thinking about solutions and engineering technology to adapt to an increasingly busy and co-located wireless population.

We have to adopt new modes of signalling beyond carving up frequency space, with individual services allocated specific channels. We have to move in a direction of allowing everyone to use all of the frequency space all of the time. The transition is almost the same as moving from two people having a conversation in a quiet room to a cocktail party where everyone is talking at once.

The electronics to operate in 'cocktail party' mode and filter out the desired signal by using the equivalent of a wireless sieve at the receiver are now available. Paradoxically, wireless communication started with spark transmitters generating signals spanning all frequencies. The interference problem was gross as the nearest transmitter to your receiver dominated. It was the arrival of electronics in the early 1900s that allowed electronic filtering to give us the channel selection we enjoy today, and provided the

Wireless today

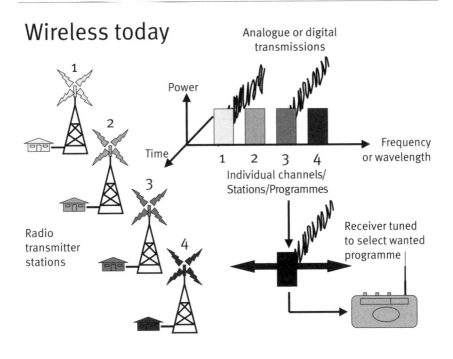

Analogue or digital
transmissions

Power

Time

Frequency
or wavelength

1 2 3 4

Individual channels/
Stations/Programmes

Radio
transmitter
stations

Receiver tuned
to select wanted
programme

Wireless tomorrow?

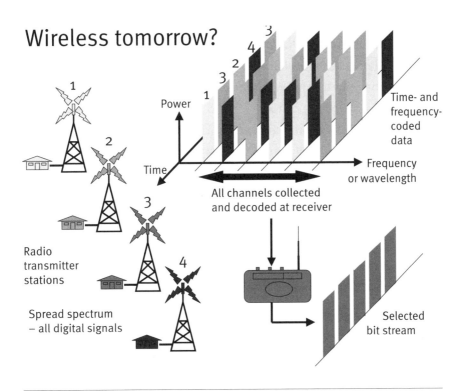

Power

Time

Time- and
frequency-
coded
data

Frequency
or wavelength

All channels collected
and decoded at receiver

Radio
transmitter
stations

Spread spectrum
– all digital signals

Selected
bit stream

foundation for all our entertainment and telecommunications services for nearly 90 years.

So we now stand to reverse history through electronic sophistication only made commercially possible by recent advances in chip technology. We can create complex digital signals that occupy a broad swath of frequency space and still filter them out at the receiver. Understanding the detail is not a simple task and is highly mathematical and convoluted, so it is probably easiest to conceive of them as thousands of contiguous micro-radio channels broadcast in parallel all at the same time. Each signal is allocated different time and micro-frequency relationships that can only be unscrambled by an a priori knowledge embedded in selected receivers.

Another way of looking at this is to see a conversation broken into channels occupying the space currently allocated to BBC Radio channels 1, 2, 3, 4 and 5. A listener would need a receiver capable of selecting all of these channels at the same time to extract and recover the conversation. This is a very simplistic explanation, but not so far from the truth. Such 'spread spectrum' systems were originally developed towards the end of WWII for secret communications beyond the detection capabilities of the enemy. It is now used in the latest generations of mobile phone and wireless LAN and is the mode of operation most likely to be ideal for the future.

Adopting this technology as the dominant mode for the future would mean the disassembling of today's radio spectrum rules in terms of frequency and power allocations. It would require new rules focused on the allocation of codes for the transmission and reception of signals for given applications, and necessary power limitations for different classes of device. For you and me as users, the big breakthrough will be an interference-free future and an unrestricted ability to communicate when and how we wish.

Byte 27
Communications Compromised

> *Technology is the name we give to stuff that doesn't work properly yet.*
>
> Douglas Adams

Is WiFi much more insecure than wireline networking? How many security clangers do you drop while on your mobile?

Of all the emotive debates generated by IT, security seems to be the one most frequently and irrationally debated. As a general rule, people's attention to security is inversely related to the actual risk, value or need. Companies pour resources into making email 100,000-fold more secure than any physical mail process, while employing temporary staff with minimal background checks, thereby leaving the security doors wide open. On the physical side it seems to be generally accepted that networks built from copper wires are reasonably secure, while those built from optical fibre are incredibly secure – and all things wireless are as leaky as a sieve.

It would seem that anything new or misunderstood immediately goes to the top of the security list without any thought or analysis. For example, most people understand that access via paired copper cable means digging it up, climbing a pole or entering a telco/cableco building, office or home. Then with the use of a pair of alligator clips it is possible to tap the line and extract any information – audio, video or data – as opportunity presents. This, by the way, is mostly far from the truth, but it will suffice for this discussion.

Optical links, on the other hand, present a far greater challenge in the minds of most, but the reality is that alligator clips for optical fibre do

Layered security/defence

Step 1	Step 2	Step 3
Border	**Authentication**	**Authorization**
Network layer	Proof of identity	Permission based
Virus scanning	Username	User permissions
Firewalls	Password	Group permissions
Intrusion detect	Public key	Admin permission
Virtual Private Nets	Tokens	Enterprise directory
Denial of service	Biometrics	Enterprise admin
Protection	Single sign on	Rule-based control
		AI reasoning

exist. By merely bending a fibre over a reasonably tight radius, light leaks out through the cladding and can be detected by a simple optical collector. So again, the recovery of audio, video or data information without a user knowing is in theory, and with delicate practice, relatively simple once physical access is achieved.

For radio, all someone basically needs is an antenna to suck information right out of the ether. Of course, if it is a microwave radio system or directed beam of some kind, it means finding the right location so you can actually intercept the waves. But if the system is an omni-directional mobile phone or wireless LAN (WLAN), or just a PC on a desk, radiating energy in every direction, it can all be picked up with relatively unsophisticated equipment. This then looks like a different and far riskier proposition.

Recently there has been a bevy of new software (for example Net-Stumbler and AirSnort) that can scan the airwaves for WLAN signals. They then list what signals are available and reveal their descriptors and vital statistics. Many programs not only list the network names and crack the Wired Equivalent Privacy (WEP) algorithmic protection currently used on WLANs, they reveal passwords and other data. The very fastest algorithms

Reported Internet security incidents

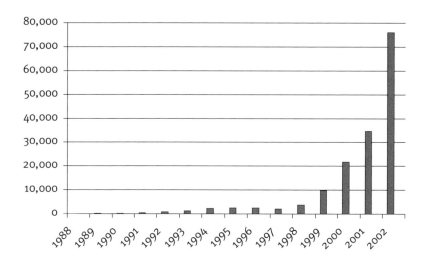

can now decode a 40-bit WEP in a matter of minutes by gathering thousands of samples of repeatedly transmitted header information.

In effect all you have to do is passively monitor one wireless transmission after another, make comparisons, and gradually the encryption key, network name and password emerge. This is all very basic but extremely effective.

Many people have been surprised that designers didn't anticipate this and only specified a 40-bit WEP key. The good news is that there is a 128-bit key option giving improved security and dictating much longer monitoring periods. In this case WLAN/WiFi remains reasonably secure for the present and represents about the same level of inconvenience to those trying to break in as a pair of copper wires.

Does any of this mean we should stop using wireless transmission? I don't think so. It would be foolish to abandon any technology on the basis of its momentary exposure to interception. The reality is that anybody wishing to intercept communication in any form over copper, fibre or wireless, has their work cut out to a modest degree. Physical access is the first priority, followed by software having the capability to decrypt the information. We should remember that the vast majority of communication on this planet

Identified Internet vulnerabilities

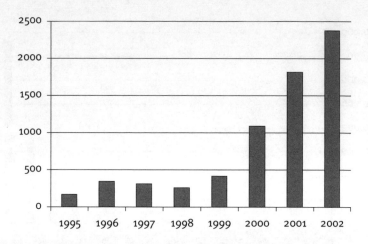

New vulnerabilities found frequently – they just increase

Source: CERT

enjoys no form of encryption or protection and the interceptions remain very small. And there is also security in numbers! Blindly intercepting data is not very effective, it is necessary to be focused in order to gain anything really useful. In general over 99.9% of human communication is of no commercial or other value to a listener – so the really good stuff is hidden in the noise. Of course this is not the case as you get closer to a specific customer or target, or as you isolate their communication channels.

When our electronic security systems become excessively expensive with protection levels that far exceed the risks accorded to the number of conversations that are overheard in a room or on a train, or indeed the number of credit cards that could be compromised after handing them to a waiter or gas station attendant, we have reached a stage when perspective has been lost. We don't often consider the ease of access to information such as printed mail in unguarded mailboxes at the end of the yard, or the ease of reading a PC screen over someone's shoulder. By comparison the eRisk is often very small.

It would be imprudent indeed not to take adequate precautions with our information and the protection of our commercial interests. The fact that wireless networks can be hacked today in terms of basic access to the network doesn't mean to say we can't increase the length of WEP keys or add further password protection and encrypt our files and folders prior to transmission. There are sufficient and more than adequate security measures available today should we choose to use them, but the reality is that most rail at the practical inconvenience, or are inherently unthinking in what they do. Also, naivety can be very risky!

If you have really important data that you do not want people to access, it's very simple: protect it before you send it. You should also remember to look over your shoulder to see who is eyeing your screen, listening to your phone call, trying your door or window, or accessing your paper mail. Security is a lot like war, you always have to have your guard up, and you have to assess the risk potential of every threat mechanism and assign your resources accordingly. What use is an ultra-secure medium if the data is printed out and then consigned to the trash to be collected by some unknown agent later?

Byte 28
Insecure Thinking

The human race seems to pay attention to security and risk in inverse proportion to the true value or the risk involved.

People will worry about their telephone and mobile phone calls being tapped and their email being intercepted, whilst installing a three-lever mortice lock on their $500k house to save $30. More foolishly they leave their car in the drive with the keys still in the ignition. Perhaps it is a basic human failing to worry about the wrong things.

A recent report cited two students at the MIT Laboratory of Computer Science, who had purchased 158 disk drives for a scrap value of $1000. Examining the drives they found over 5000 credit card numbers, numerous medical reports, corporate and financial information from a myriad of sources, personal email and an unmeasured amount of pornography. It seems that individuals and corporations just remove hard drives and scrap systems without taking the trouble to recover or clean out their data. Had they been dishonest, these students had recovered sufficient information to keep them in the blackmail and coercion business for decades for only $1000. Instead they published their results in a professional journal (*IEEE Security and Privacy*, Jan/Feb 03) to bring this lunatic and irresponsible practice to light.

They concluded that buying any ten drives on the used market sees a 30% chance of finding confidential and useful information. This is staggering, a huge opportunity for dishonesty, and a great advertisement for human fallibility!

Hard drives are expanding their capability far faster than RAM or data processing, and people are increasingly installing additional hard drives or

Deaths/1,000,000 people

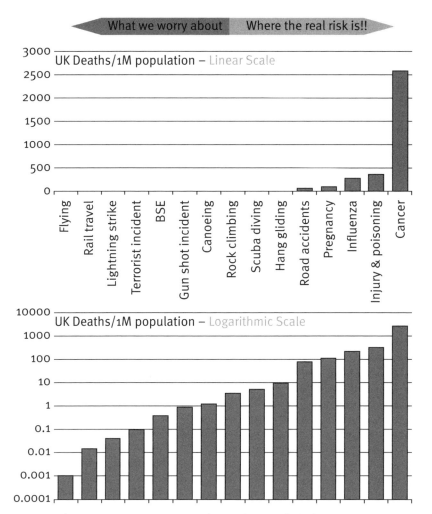

The perception and reality of risk

Both graphs are identical but use two different scales.

The upper graph is linear and gives a true perspective of relative risk.

The lower graph is a log (non-linear) scale and gives the full detail.

Look at the difference between flying and influenza – it is ›100,000 to 1.

So what do people worry about? Nothing!

eCommerce worries

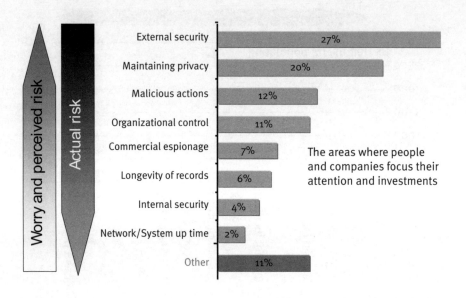

upgrading before they trade in their old box for new. In just one year the standard PC purchased on the high street has moved from a 60GByte hard drive to 120GByte at more or less the same price. But 160 and 200GByte are also available and soon they will be the norm. The opportunity presented to the criminal is getting bigger very fast!

There is plenty of software available to scrub and clean out hard drives before discarding them. But if they have become such a security risk that a software scrub still leaves you feeling nervous, it is well worth locking old drives into a secure safe. Alternatively, data eradication with a large hammer works well and ensures 100% security.

The students found that 129 of the 158 drives purchased were still functional and 28 had seen no attempt to erase any information. One drive that had been recovered from an ATM contained one year's worth of financial transactions recorded. This is insane, irresponsible and a far greater risk than online examination by some unseen electronic burglar.

It would appear that most people do not realize that when they delete a document or a folder, it only removes the document header and the data remains on the disk undamaged. To remove the data requires a secure delete application of which there are numerous on the market including: Cyber-Scrub, DataGone, Eraser, SecureClean and Wipe. Defragging will achieve a similar end, but it is worth checking by using an un-delete utility or disk doctor/toolbox type application before discarding. My personal policy is to retain all hard drives in a fireproof safe. After five years my inclination is to put them under the hammer and dispatch them as scrap rather than trying to re-use. After five years they offer an insignificant storage capacity compared to their time of purchase.

I have no idea why people and organizations are so lax about security, but there is a tendency to assume that someone else is taking care of the problem. The reality is that we all have a responsibility not only to look after our own information and data, but that of those around us too. If you are using a PC on a broadband network you need to install a hardware or software firewall to prevent attacks and potential damage.

There seem to be thousands of Web crawlers out there, and I see tens of hits on my home network every day. For corporate networks with even more bandwidth and a huge potential for meaningful theft and damage, I suspect it is even greater. If you have no firewall I recommend that you install one, and if you have a firewall it is worth keeping the software up to date. Cyber-criminals never sleep and never stop in their efforts to encroach into our data world.

To date there has not been a single instance of anyone, anywhere having their credit card number intercepted directly over the net. Every recorded instance of card crime involves the intervention of a human being at the beginning or end of the process, or some embedded Trojan horse software, and of course the straight cyber attack, gaining access to a hard drive with non-encrypted files. It is seems that looking over a shoulder at an ATM, or taking a copy of the card and signature at a gas station or restaurant, or some spoof transaction are the favoured routes to our money. The discarding of hard drives full of data or indeed any other document, electronic or paper gives the dishonest a wonderful opportunity to perpetuate even more card crimes.

So far the net appears to be the safest environment we have created for financial transactions, but like our homes and automobiles we ought not to jeopardize that safety by being foolish. Discarding or trading old machines and hard drives needs a professional touch. And we ought not to use plain text for our valuable information – passwords, accounts and transactions – we really should use the security tools to hand. After all, no one would sell a wardrobe whilst it still contained all their clothes with cheque book and credit cards in the jacket pocket – would they?

Byte 29
Wear, Where, Were-ables

Telecommunications seems to be doing for the travel industry what the PC did for the paperless office!

Compared to the 100 years it took for the telephone to become a universal business tool, the rise of computing power in the past 50 years, the PC over the past 20, and in particular the mobile phone in the last 12, seems miraculous. Even more miraculous is the arrival of the Internet and the mere six years it took to commercialize, which has seen more social and commercial change than anyone guessed or imagined.

In just 12 years 59 million people purchased 90 million mobiles in the UK. Today there are 45 million operational mobiles. Across the planet, the story is often even more extreme, and in the second world the mobile phone is often the only phone. No forecaster, engineer, marketing or sales executive guessed so many would pay so much for so little! It appears that convenience and mobility overrides all consideration of call quality. In fact, doing everything on the move seems to be our preference.

I travel the planet with a 2.5G mobile that allows me to communicate from anywhere, with anyone, anytime, at an acceptable cost. I conduct business independent of a fixed office or continent. Whilst the power of my laptop has seen my productivity advance tenfold in ten years, my mobile phone has seen my travel itinerary become increasingly frantic. Telecommunications seems to be doing for the travel industry what the PC did for the paperless office!

We tend to think of wearing technology as the wristwatch, PDA, mobile phone, pager and hearing aid. Many see wearables as walking the streets looking like the back of a PC. In my view it will be a subtle migration.

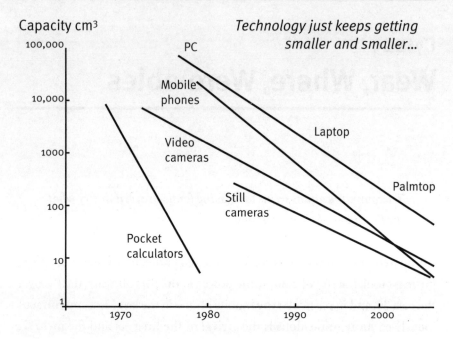

People already talk into free space with the mobile phone in their pocket and headset in their ear. Gameboy users wear head-up displays. Most of us wear a wristwatch, and many a Walkman, Discman or MP3 player – and I occasionally wear a GPS wristwatch!

Wearables are already with us in many forms and gaining more belt, pocket and body space. We will soon see barcodes on our clothing, driving license, passport and credit cards, replaced by wireless transponders – RFID tags. It is also likely that we will choose to carry our complete electronic medical record with us at all times. But adding GPS to all our mobile devices will be profound. In an instant we will locate a container on a ship, a stolen vehicle, an accident or emergency location, someone in need of urgent medical attention, not to mention our younger children. And we can soon expect to enter a room or building to find a message, metaphorically hanging in space for us, only to be accessed when we visit that location.

As I travel I want to be assured that I am safe and secure, and able to communicate at will. I would like my personal information made instantly available to streamline all physical processes including security, access and purchases. RFID tags on everything will make this possible and save vast amounts of time and money.

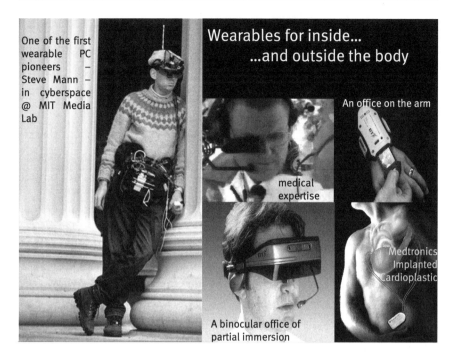

One of the first wearable PC pioneers – Steve Mann – in cyberspace @ MIT Media Lab

Wearables for inside...
...and outside the body

An office on the arm

medical expertise

Medtronics Implanted Cardioplastic

A binocular office of partial immersion

The key element in this increasingly wearable future is wireless communication between the multiple devices we wear and the outside world. The Bluetooth standard has been developed for the former, and 3G for the latter, and more recently a new contender for both has appeared in the form of the IEEE802.11 (WiFi) standards. So with a myriad of intelligent items we can buy and wear, we may arrive at the wearable computer by instalments.

It is likely that MP3 and mobile phones will merge with a GPS and PDA facility. This will enable communication between health monitoring and security elements plus our clothing tags to compute our needs and help with purchases and transportation. At the other extreme, all of these items may come ready assembled in our clothing, fully wired and ready to go, in the form of a vest, shirt or jacket.

The key question is, how is the limited radio spectrum going to cope? Fortunately we have used <10% of the frequency spectrum available. Between 30 and 300GHz almost none of the spectrum is used because molecular resonances make it difficult to communicate over significant distances. For example, at 270GHz communication is limited to ~100m. This mitigates for a future pico-cells – exactly what is required!

With conventional mobiles the communication cells span 1–25km, to cope with the density of handsets in most city and rural locations. But as the number of mobile devices rises we will need individual cells for the human body, car, room, home, office, building, hotel, campus, street, village, town, and so on. What is required to achieve this? Only the allocation of unused frequency space, power-limiting specifications to keep radio operation safe and interference free, and smart software. The good news is that short distance communication also mitigates for low power and, along with mobile phones, most new devices adjust the transmitter power so that it is just sufficient for each application.

A long time ago I speculated on a pair of spectacles that would extend my visible frequency range into the UV and IR. That was realized by night vision devices and image intensifiers. The next step might be to go down the frequency range so we can see below 300GHz. Now that would be interesting! We all give off heat as infra-red radiation, and soon that will be overtaken by radio frequency radiation, and it will make for a very interesting picture!

Byte 30
How Many Mobile Phones Do You Need?

Communications should be simple, right? There are plenty of factors meaning it isn't always so …

I'm standing on a New York street corner observing an archetypal American policeman. He is wearing over 30lbs of hardware around his waist, plus a bullet-proof vest and a yard-stick in one hand. On his waist are: a pistol, several ammunition clips, mace, handcuffs, and two very large (weapon-like) walkie-talkies. So it is with some surprise I watch him reach for, and use at length, a standard mobile phone.

I wait until he has finished his conversation and then cannot resist the temptation to stroll over and ask him why he is using a mobile phone. The response is a curt, New York: 'because it works'. I enquired as to whether the walkie-talkies worked and 'not all of the time,' was his reply. Interesting!

Just a few weeks before this NY encounter I was up in the Boulder, Colorado area and got an earful from the local sheriff's department on the pros and cons of analogue and digital mobile systems. The Rocky Mountains are less friendly than any city to wireless systems and, it seems, to any digital system. The binary nature of digital systems means that they work or they don't, with very little in between. With the old analogue systems, performance can appear to be far more robust as failure always has, as a precursor, a worsening signal-to-noise ratio; that is, reception gradually gets noisier. Of course there are a few more subtleties related to the frequency of operation, which tends to be higher for digital than analogue radio, plus multi-path propagation, but the broad result is a noisier signal decline for analogue.

The key outcome for the police department has been a reversion to the old technology because it works! But, curiously, I seem to have mobile

Mobile phone users forecast

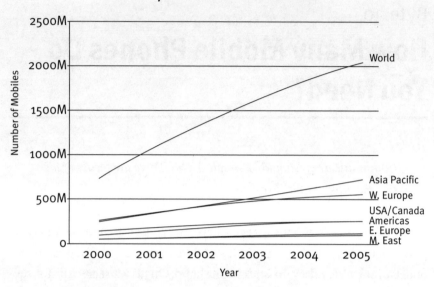

Source: http://www.emc-database.com/website.nsf/index/pro11030#this-page

(GSM) telephone coverage almost everywhere I travel in Colorado, whether on the plane, across the desert, in the forests and mountains, the coverage is excellent given the nature of the terrain. So I suspect that it is likely that more than one sheriff's department in the US are also using mobile phones as the primary or secondary means of communication!

A mobile phone comes off a production line at less than $20 while the police walkie-talkie costs ten times as much. The military, of course, pay an even higher price (~10× more again) for man pack radios, which can also lack the performance and resilience of a standard mobile phone. This all raises the question as to why the emergency services, police and military do not adopt the cellular mobile standard. This could reduce their communications costs, while advancing their abilities in one fell swoop.

Simply allocating a few channels of the civil cellular network for exclusive government use, plus software to override other cellular users in cases of national emergency or war would see a far greater capability than enjoyed today. In addition, battlefield or warzone communication could easily be adapted to use mobile cellular base stations which, if necessary, could be linked to HF radio and satellites for a wider range of communication.

During every terrorist incident or outbreak of war, communications between multiple services from different countries turns out to be a key stumbling block. The coordination of our military services is hampered by the very technology that should make it easier. The enemy, however, is using a mobile phone network and, as a result, has far more efficient and rapid communication. It might be that vested interests are preventing the obvious step towards integration of communication for all our services, but I prefer the cock-up or SNAFU explanation.

There is a major opportunity here for what I would call 'bridgeware'. This technology would allow the devices used by our police, emergency services and military to hop from one available network to another, providing both voice and data communication. This is not rocket science but it is different.

People in the communications industry often talk about convergence. As far as I can see there is absolutely no evidence of convergence anywhere, any time in our past or present. The reality is that we are introducing more networks and network types, more protocols, operating systems, applications and devices by the day. We have never seen a period of convergence and we are not seeing a period of convergence now. We are witnessing a divergence on a par with the Cambrian explosion of life itself, some 500 million years ago.

I have no doubt in my mind that there will ultimately be a collapse in every respect to a small number of network types, operating systems, applications and devices – only not yet. Until that happens we are going to continue to see one period after another of people having communication difficulties in companies, corporations and the services. The simplest step is to adopt the most prevalent signalling standard and technology at the lowest cost that will do the job.

The vast majority of humanity (except those living in North America) enjoy mobile communication capability that is the envy of the military and police – and Dick Tracey for that matter! Like the New York cop, the vast majority of the people in government services are purchasing their own mobile phone and setting up their own sub-networks to bypass something that doesn't work quite as well as it should.

This could be the start of a new regime. Perhaps companies and governments will eventually withdraw from the purchase and supply of mobile communications, as we all vote with our feet and purchase our own.

Byte 31

The Right Technology For The Right Job

No one has successfully transmitted significant amounts of data over power cables.

For a decade now business plans have arrived on my desk in increasing numbers, but only a very small percentage find their way to commercial success. What is remarkable is that I see very little correlation between plans. There is however a major exception where the same plan seems to arrive on my desk every year. Each time it is presented as revolutionary and groundbreaking, and is usually backed by significant amounts of investment. But it is always the same technology, and it is always as flawed and as misconceived as the original I first saw a decade ago. News reports are often included to amplify the case along the following lines:

> *'The XYZ Company is proud to report that broadband Internet trials are underway using a groundbreaking technology that will revolutionize radio, TV, cable TV, Internet and data services to the home. Existing electricity power cables in your street, city and state, can supply all of your digital services at speeds of up to 50Mbit/s. Extensive laboratory trials have proven this technology, and testing with customers is at an early stage. If fully successful a commercial rollout is planned within the next three months.'*

It is then customary to include a CEO interview that says something along these lines:

'All the technical obstacles have been overcome, the technology is now proven, stable and economic, and we are in a position to revolutionize the last mile. We also predict that this technology will see the demise of the telco in the next decade ...'

It is not unusual for partner companies to keep their names secret in anticipation of further announcements to be made later that year. The technical press always grab this story and seem convinced that it is true and we are on the verge of yet another last mile revolution that really will damage the telcos. But within the twelve months following the press announcements, the companies involved generally slink off into the night or quietly announce that they are ceasing the trial after the first few hundreds or thousands of homes have been connected. We are reassured that this is usually due to some political or economic developments, or because some alternative technology has been discovered. It then goes very quiet and nothing more is heard.

I wouldn't find this so upsetting if it only happened once, but to my knowledge there have been at least five or six attempts. If only the people involved would visit my office I could save them a small fortune. At a modest estimate something of the order of $200M has been expended to date and no one has been successful in transmitting significant amounts of data over power cables to the home. And I can guarantee no one will get this technology to work as originally advertised. It might be appealing and economically attractive at first glance, but I'm afraid the basic laws of physics cannot be dismissed or overcome. For anyone contemplating the waste of another $5–30M, here is my 'don't do it' shortlist:

1   Copper cables supplying our electrical power employ low-grade plastic that is unfriendly to high-frequency signals and the absorption per unit length is very high. This alone precludes transmission of high-speed data over significant distances. Moreover, there are multiple transformers and power meters that are also unfriendly to high speed data signals.

2   Power cables are not physically symmetrical and they are therefore very effective antennas. They radiate high-frequency energy to become a

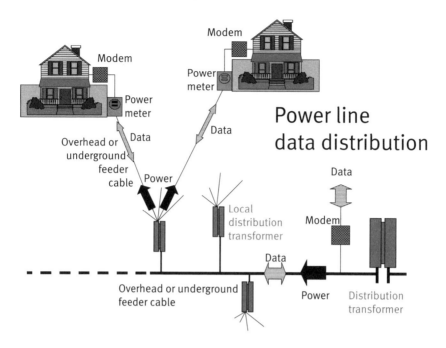

source of interference to all other technologies in their vicinity including TV, radio, wireless LANs, taxis, emergency services. By reciprocity they also suck in energy from every local radio source available, which further degrades data signals.

3   As signals propagate along any cable they become weaker, but in the case of power cables the switching transients from washing machines, refrigerators, vacuum cleaners, electric drills, light switches and other appliances are huge and do not decay at the same rate, and the received data signals are often swamped.

4   Switching transients and flashovers within power grids themselves are created by generators going on and off line, dynamic load sharing, circuit switching, lightening, fault and maintenance work. All of these sources induce massive transients that are very visible for both the source and customer end of the power cables and totally swamp low level data signals.

5   Cable joints and the on/off nature of electrical appliance create large load changes and signal reflection points. This creates a dynamic echo

environment where the transmitted signal is further corrupted – but in a dynamic and unpredictable manner.

6   The nature of (3 and 4) is to create blanking periods of zero signal reception which precludes any real time services – radio, TV, telephone, games = voice, vision, control and interaction.

This is a very short disaster list that says this technology will not deliver what it might at first appear to promise. The real nail in the coffin is as follows: telephone and cables were designed to carry far higher frequencies than power cables and in every aspect offer superior performance for all data applications. More recently, wireless technology has become so low cost and high performance that signal processing requirements for data over power cables, even if it were possible, would be prohibitively expensive in comparison. And in many locations the power companies have installed optical fibre along their power lines for telemetry concerned with the control of power distribution. Because their data requirements are so meagre huge amounts of bandwidth are available. So it does make sense for wireless technology to be used at that end point, in a distribution mode to attack the last mile.

Contrary to a widely held belief, all the technology necessary to transform the local loop is to hand and no-hope solutions such as data over power cables should be seen as red herrings. So please will the next candidate thinking of sending me another business plan with a revolutionary technology that will exploit power cables please employ someone who understands Maxwell's equations and data transmission.

Byte 32
Network Power

No doubt about it, we seem to be moving from a world of concentrated skill and expertise to a world of distributed ignorance.

Only 200 years ago it was possible to be a leading engineer and zoologist at the same time. Even 50 years ago it was possible to understand the fine-grain detail of the telephone or television network, or indeed all the inner workings of an automobile, but today no one knows everything about almost anything. No single human mind understands and contains the full design and operational detail of even the simplest of aircraft. The knowledge required to create materials, turn them into the component parts and mould them into a complete system is way beyond the capacity of any one human.

Should we be shaking our heads in despair at the demise of the polymath? Perhaps, but then again perhaps not! The upside to the technology that saw their demise has, in part, allowed us all to become more powerful. We may have created a sea of ignorance, but we have also opened up windows of capability that we could not have imagined even 20 years ago.

The power of networking is something that most people do not contemplate and few understand. For example, if we take a broadcast network, as in radio and TV, we see a single transmitter with a number of receivers. If these receivers number 'N' then the information flow is at best proportional to N/2. But, in practice, not all of the receivers are on all of the time and not all listeners or viewers are paying attention. So the information flow is always $\leq$ N/2.

In complete contrast the telephone network sees a phenomenal increase in the information flow and connectivity. The growth in the connections of

Network laws

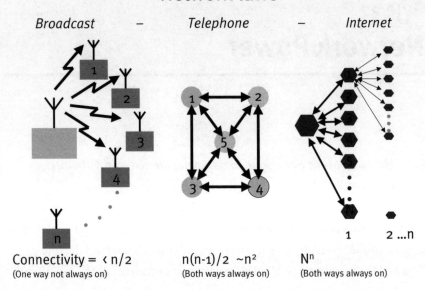

Broadcast – *Telephone* – *Internet*

Connectivity = < n/2
(One way not always on)

$n(n-1)/2 \sim n^2$
(Both ways always on)

N^n
(Both ways always on)

How many friends do you have...
...how many people do you know?

Separation => People you know

0	=>	30	0	=>	300
1	=>	900	1	=>	90,000
2	=>	27,000	2	=>	27,000,000
3	=>	810,000	3	=>	8,100,000,000
4	=>	24,300,000			
5	=>	729,000,000			
6	=>	21,870,000,000			

If you have 30 people on your address book then in one click you can reach/infect 900. In two clicks this goes to 27,000. In just six clicks you have infected every computer on the net. If however you have 300 people, then it only take three clicks to achieve that outcome. If we all had >1000 contacts in our address books it would only take two clicks. This is exponential networking ... this is why viruses and memes spread so fast and we can now be so creative!

From the few to the many...

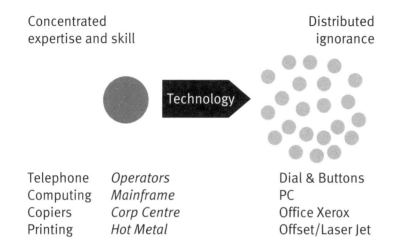

Concentrated expertise and skill		Distributed ignorance
Telephone	*Operators*	Dial & Buttons
Computing	*Mainframe*	PC
Copiers	*Corp Centre*	Office Xerox
Printing	*Hot Metal*	Offset/Laser Jet

Distributed ignorance wins!

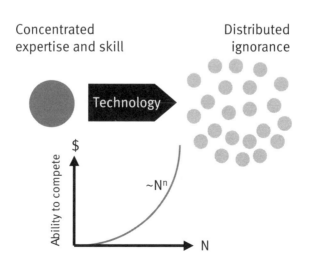

the telephone with the number of nodes 'N' now goes up as $N*(N-1)/2$ and as N becomes very large, the information flow goes up as $(N^2)/2$. Whilst this is just a modest change in network architecture, with every node being both transmitter and receiver, it has led to changes in society that no one ever imagined, and even more so with the addition of mobility.

An even bigger change in network power, and society, has occurred with the arrival of the Internet. Here the connectivity is far more complex and powerful than the broadcast and telephone networks that preceded it. Now we have to think of a web of hyperlinks or the concatenation of address books. The Internet expands in an exponential form N^n, as explained below.

Probably the easiest way to visualize the increase in network power is to consider a sneeze and the spread of an airborne virus. One person in a public place sneezes and five people are infected, a day later, they sneeze and in turn they infect five more. Day by day, the infection increases exponentially at 5^N where N is the number of days.

Another way of looking at this is the spread of computer viruses, which accelerate across our planet at an even greater rate than a biological virus. Suppose you have 30 people in your address book and you get a virus. Within six mouse clicks you have inflicted copies of that virus on the entire computer population of the planet ($30^6 = 0.73Bn$). If on the other hand you have 300 people in your address book, just four clicks will do the trick ($300^4 = 8.1Bn$). And remember that $1Bn = 1,000,000,000$ – about the same number as the population of India.

As with the human population, the degree of separation between computers is very small. If all computers can connect to just another 30, then the degree of separation is only five. For 300 it is 3. This is based on the assumption that the virus is passed on between computers where exactly the same numbers are available in each address book, which is a gross simplification, but I'm sure you get the idea.

Of course we should worry about viruses of all kinds and the spread of physical diseases and the software capable of crippling our networks. We should also focus on the fact that we are looking at a means of communication, information access and knowledge-sharing on a scale that we have never been able to achieve before.

The reason a world of distributed ignorance wins over a world of concentrated skill and capability is that a generic education allows us to take knowledge, advice and capability from anywhere on the planet and turn it to our advantage. This model is far more powerful than being a specialist in the topic of Lithuanian pottery or the crafting of wood. I am not decrying the skill and ability of people to process raw material and do things that are useful and powerful in their own right. Each of us will no doubt profess to be an expert in something, and will attempt to hold on to some basic skill that we value and indeed may be valued by society at large. But we also need to be able to turn our hand to things where we have no natural ability or knowledge. In that sense, the Internet and this new mode of networking allows us to do just that.

All of this raises the spectre of a new paradigm for all organizations. Throughout my life I have watched and have been subject to people who have sought to be powerful by controlling and limiting the flow of information that they alone posses. I tend to label such people as control freaks as they very often seem to have only that skill and ability.

In this new millennium each of us has to adopt a different mode of operation; to give away, broadcast, make available all our knowledge and information in order to contribute to the broader objectives of our organizations. We should not seek to be powerful and to control; we should seek to be influential and to contribute by sharing everything we reasonably can across this new network of contacts that is just a click away.

Byte 33
DIY Networking

The IT world has been a contest between DIY and the Do IT For Me.
I think DIY is about to take over!

The 1950s saw an explosive growth in the USA TV network, with some communities beyond the reach of their nearest transmitter and unable to receive a reasonable TV picture. It was not economically viable to install sufficient transmitters to service every small community and alternative solutions had to come from within these far-flung communities. So, a few frustrated but knowledgeable individuals set about building towers with high gain antennas and amplifiers to capture sufficient signal. They then distributed home-to-home using coaxial cable and electronic amplifiers. This was the birth of the Community Antenna TV (CATV) systems, which ultimately became CAble TV (CATV) in the 1980s.

The last decade has seen a rapid growth of the mobile phone network, hi-fi, video, games, surround sound and PCs, all based on DIY purchase, installation and maintenance. What is critical is the speed of deployment. In less than 12 years the planet's mobile phones have overtaken the fixed-line phone population, installed for over 100 years. And the reason? It was largely in the control of the consumer and not the supplier of the service. Can you imagine what would have happened if the TV broadcasters who created the programme material had also developed, manufactured, sold, installed and maintained our TVs? I think we can safely assume that none of us would own one! In contrast, the telephone companies installed all the wires to homes over a 100-year period, and mostly precluded homeowners from doing their own network wiring. So the IT world has been a contest between DIY and the Do IT For Me, and I think DIY is about to take over and win!

B2B activity enjoys high-speed networks across corporate LANS and has expanded world trade whilst simultaneously realizing vast operational savings. In contrast, B2C has realized an insignificant fraction of its full potential. The principal reason? A lack of bandwidth to the home! However, P2P networking has emerged out of the consumer frustration and is now responsible for more bit exchange than home Internet connections. The bandwidth is huge and free, and fuelling a huge grey economy of games and MP3 music dominated by illegal copies propagating for free.

The key question is: when will we all get significant bandwidth to the home, and what will the technology be? Will DSL technology save the day? I think not! This is the last gasp of the ancient copper network and it increasingly looks like a band-aid solution. It is wholly underpowered even before it is deployed. A 256K/bit or 2Mbit/s download capability may have been a reasonable prospect a decade ago, but with the advance of PC technology has seen a huge gap widen between the two domains. In Korea a significant proportion of the population enjoy 10Mbit/s to the home, and some are moving up to 50Mbit/s. This is over 100× faster than EU services to the home and 50× faster than those in the USA – and 1000× faster than a dial-up modem.

Copper is a static technology that has changed very little in the last 50 years. The cables were originally designed for speech signals and now transport data 1000× faster. In contrast, computers, optical fibre and data networks have realized performance improvements >>1,000,000× in 20 years. Moreover, there is no foreseeable slowdown in the rate of advance expected for at least the next 20 years. So the copper and glass paradigms are entirely out of kilter, with copper cables offering severe limits to any further progress. What can be done? The good news is that much of the local loop cabling is installed in buried ducts that obviate the need for huge amounts of civil engineering. So installing optical fibre is a straightforward proposition. Fibre to the home was first shown to be economically viable on new or replacement installations in 1986 when most could not imagine a need for connections beyond those provided by copper. Only the vested interests of the existing local loop community, coupled with spurious and ill-informed economic studies, precluded any significant (if any) rollout.

Wireless LAN (WiFi) in the local loop

All homes with wireless systems send out a
limited-range search signal, hopping house
to house looking for a
broadband hub.

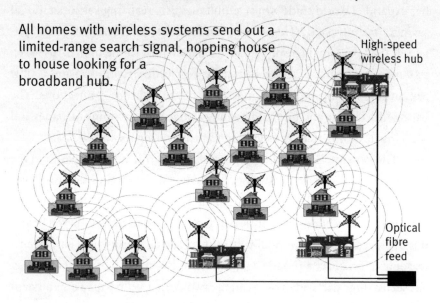

High-speed
wireless hub

Optical
fibre
feed

Wireless LAN (WiFi) in the local loop

Shortest hop, or dual hop routings are established to give high
speed connections at very low cost – network automatically
reorganizes in the event of a node failing or being switched off

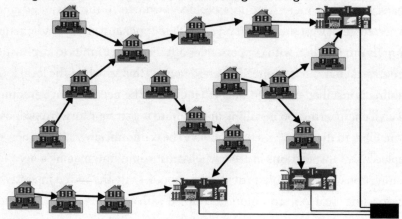

Rate of adoption – first four years

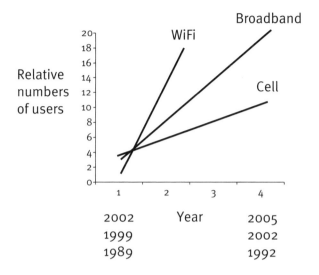

Today we see the commerce, creativity and productivity of countries crippled by a lack of adequate road and rail transport compounded by no bandwidth to the home and office. Economies are being impacted by the lack of bandwidth and the inability to connect. Could satellites provide a significant alternative? No! They will never be able to provide a significant amount of capacity compared with fixed cables. In their entire history satellites have made little impact in telecommunications, other than in broadcast and the accessing of countries and locations where it is difficult to install cables. Right now the easiest and interim last-mile technology to install is actually line-of-site radio, which can deliver bandwidths >10 Mbit/s.

For the network companies the most pressing problem is the lack of an economic business model. The fundamental problem stems from the point economics employed, it is extremely difficult to justify the installation of anything new when you have an established base of copper cables. This is especially true if the copper was paid for a long time ago. Yet if we factor in the cost of ownership and new-install costs, then fibre and radio are very competitive. Copper demands a huge amount of ongoing attention, with thousands of repair crews dedicated to repairing damage caused by water and corrosion. Fibre is impervious to water and can be programmed remotely because of its huge bandwidth capability. In short, physical re-routings are no longer required. The scale of the problem is massive in terms of the number of people required and the time to install, and an echo of the late 1800s, when the decision to build a massive railroad infrastructure had to be taken despite the riverboat and canal owner lobby. The reality is that there is little chance any nation will see a complete change over to optical fibre in the local loop in anything less than a ten-year period – at a cost of > $10Bn.

What are the general public to do in order to get adequate Internet connectivity and to continue the growth of the business to consumer boom? The self-install of very short-range wireless networks is an obvious solution and one that communities are capable of completing with minimal technical skill. History may repeat itself with WLANs echoing the earlier CATV. Today Manhattan has over 12,000 self-installed WLAN/WiFi systems that could potentially offer contiguous service across complete city blocks, and much of London is the same. All that is required is the legislation necessary for the resale of existing broadband capacity. Install WiFi at every broadband node and in every home and office and immediately many more can get access and, moreover, the connectivity is significantly broadened with coverage spreading like a virus infection. But like an infection it will cost nothing to disperse, as all the nodes are self-financed, installed and maintained!

Byte 34
Stupid Entertainment

As the music industry takes drastic action to block illegal downloads of MP3 files, will it do any good?

Can you imagine having the money and power to purchase a vast fleet of automobiles to fill up all the parking lots, roads and freeways so you could purposely inconvenience the rest of humanity? Alternatively perhaps being able to clog the mail system with bogus letters and parcels? Alternatively, how about paying huge numbers of people to fill all the train and aircraft seats to create great inconvenience to those who really need to travel! Now wouldn't that be really stupid! And surely it would soon be declared an illegal act.

On the net we have several companies paid by the music industry to clog up sites and servers with bogus MP3 files in an attempt to crush peer-to-peer file sharing. It isn't illegal, yet, but it ought to be! It might even turn out to be mildly inconvenient for the vast majority of the net population. Why are they doing this? It all started with Napster, and the continued attempts of the music industry to destroy a new era of freedom and stifle the creation of new business models.

I am all in favour of artists, producers and distributors getting their due reward for their creativity and labours. But ignoring or opposing change made possible by new technology is very dangerous. Some of the most greedy, desperate and stupid people (a very dangerous combination) I ever met are employed in the entertainment sector. They always deny the new until it is killing them. From wax cylinder, to plastic disc, magnetic tape, CD, VHS, DVD, analogue to digital, these people have been dragged kicking

CDs – online and peer-to-peer ($)

	Traditional	Digital	Peer-to-peer
Marketing	0.75	0.75	0.75
Manufacture	1.00	0.10	0.10
Distribution	2.30	0.10	0.10
Royalty – Producer	0.70	0.70	0.70
Retailer	6.60	1.50	0.00
Royalty – Artist	1.25	4.00	0.00
Label profit	5.30	10.85	0.00
Total	$ 18.00	$ 18.00	$ 1.65

and screaming across every technological and market threshold by their customers – the consumer.

Hollywood spent millions of dollars trying to stop VHS – and today that technology earns them most of their annual $10Bn income. The record companies similarly tried to stop audio-tape recording, and subsequently made a fortune out of cassettes. And so each advantageous technology has been fought and forestalled right up to the present day. Today it is MP3 and the ripping and stripping of CDs that is seen as the big evil.

But is MP3 merely payback time for decades of ripping off artists and public by the music industry? This may be hard justice for making us buy 15

Books – old and new

	Traditional	Digital	Change
Production	$ 4.80	$ 0.00	-100%
Editing	0.45	0.45	0%
Royalties	1.45	1.45	0%
Marketing	1.25	1.25	0%
Sales commission	0.83	0.48	-40%
Total	$ 8.03	$ 3.63	-55%
Publisher profit	$ 1.97	$ 2.37	-20%
Distributor cost	$ 10.00	$ 6.00	-40%
Distributor profit	$ 4.00	$ 4.00	0%
Shop price	$14.00	$10.00	-29%

Music and movie downloads/month

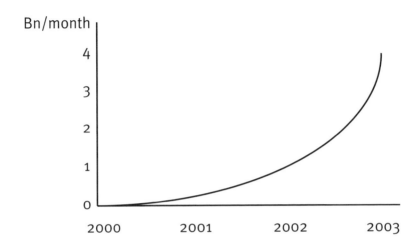

second-rate tracks we don't like to get the two we really want? I hope this is not the case. It is in no one's interest to destroy the entertainment industry. Equally, it is not in anyone's interest if those in the industry are trying to get a PhD in stupidity! It is clearly time for a new distribution chain and a new business model to complement the newest technology.

We all watched in amazement as the music industry decided not to embrace the Napster concept. It could have seized the opportunity to create a new style business of online music sales that would have been supported by most. Instead they attacked and killed the opportunity, and now they have 40M Napsters they cannot control or kill! But they stumble on blindly, lashing out at every advance and change as if it is all inherently evil.

Their next move was even more stupid in the development of the content-controlled CD costing millions for deployment, and follow-on damage. Here, CD software allows hi-fi operation and disables all PC applications. The kids got around this by re-digitizing the tracks by linking hi-fi output to PC audio input. They then got refunds on the original CD because it didn't work correctly! The next workaround was even simpler and more ingenious. By simply running a felt tip pen around the outer edge of a CD, the control tracks can be disabled. A $0.10 pen could overcome $M of development costs – I like it! (That particular trick won't work for much longer though – see www.silicon.com/a55293.)

In the meantime the movie industry has also been hard at work with the regionalization of DVD distribution. If you buy a DVD from the USA it will refuse to play in the UK or Southeast Asia and vice versa. Now what possible reason could be offered for this practice? It can only be price, content and release control. Why as users would this be to our advantage? It can't possibly be! As a frequent traveller I buy DVDs wherever I happen to be on the planet – and what fun this creates.

On my home DVDs I took care to purchase models that have already been chipped or, alternatively, can be easily software programmed to adapt to any region. If you don't do this it can mean additional expense to get the necessary hardwiring completed and/or software installed. Increasingly the box-makers have responded to customer demand for source transparency and fully functional multiregional players are gradually becoming the norm. Customers = 1, Hollywood = 0. Game over – I think!

On my laptop and desktop machines I have DVD drives and players built in which automatically flip from region to region standard a limited number of times and then declare that they have been frozen in the last setting and that's that! There are several very simple get-outs here. First you can reinstall the software and start again – messy but easy. Second, you can install multiple players – one for each of the three regions – very easy and convenient. Third there are software workarounds and patches that bypass all this and allow your player to be multiregional. Customers = 1, Hollywood = 0. Game over!

So what will the entertainment industry try next? They are currently lobbying Congress in the USA, and getting some support, to have hardware protection made mandatory in all electronic devices in order to prevent all forms of CD and DVD copying. How they think this will be enforced on a global scale beats me. And a workaround for such technology? I don't think it will take more than about a day!

Of course it could get much worse, there seems to be an unlimited source of stupidity available! How about embedded software on CDs and

DVDs that worms its way into servers and individual PCs to destroy applications and operating systems, and/or lock up CD/DVD drives? I suspect they are already working on it.

The entertainment industry really ought to start thinking. The companies they have employed to flood the net with bogus MP3 files are being bombarded by bogus sign-ups to pornography sites and denial of service attacks. I suspect that this is just the beginning of David and Goliath-style story. The entertainment industry is Goliath and there are over 400 million Davids. In the biblical story David was either lucky, an excellent shot, or had the benefit of divine guidance. We, the consumer, don't need any of these, with over 400 million slings, one of us is bound to bring Goliath down.

Byte 35
Net Police

The lawless are slowing down our communications. Would an Internet police force be the answer?

For the past 15 years we have enjoyed a growing web of rich content and communications. Despite the madness of the dot-com bust, the freedom of communication and new business engendered by this revolution has been huge, with $Tns saved in the B2B arena and the same potential in B2C, if only we could all get bandwidth at any time in any location.

At the height of this great and unrivalled success it is therefore paradoxical that the freedom we have quickly learned to enjoy and exploit is threatened by that same freedom. Along with many other individuals and organizations, I can report that I am seeing a tidal wave of spam mail and other disruptive action causing an increasing loss of productivity. In a few months I have gone from a few spam emails a week to over 20 per day.

Some of this email is legitimate advertising, which I can easily filter and reject. But the most troublesome seems to come from the sex industry, where the level of deviousness beggars belief. To date these people always send a JPEG or MPEG plus EXE attachments, with promises of very nice pictures, or very nice games, *which I would be foolish to open*. Then there is the virus brigade that use email, MS Word and other file formats to spread their unwanted grief. But most recently it has been works of art for sale, miraculous money-making schemes, offers of new business services, and vacation opportunities. Of course, there are also those not-to-be-missed financial opportunities emanating out of Nigeria. Spam just seems to be arriving thicker and faster.

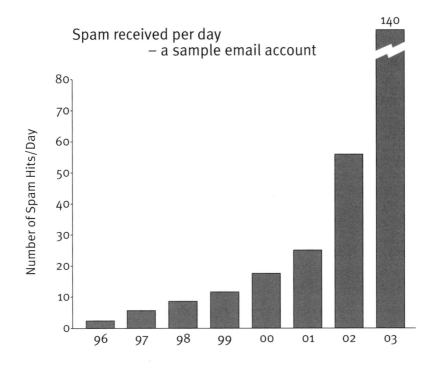

Spam received per day
 – a sample email account

What is the cost of all this? For the past 12 months the best estimate for the US economy alone is around $9Bn with the EU around $3Bn. The total for the planet is most probably in excess of $20Bn.

So far, I have been able to cope with this unwanted tide of trouble, and so have my companies. But I see SMEs and giant corporations gradually adopting draconian solutions that will ultimately cripple much of the old WWW culture of freedom. Instead of being able to walk in to any company and find (DHCP) LAN access freely available, company-by-company this facility is being closed down. Just being able to do email as a visitor, or do private email as an employee, or indeed having unbridled access to Web sites, is gradually being denied. As a result, productivity and creativity gains are being lost and economies disadvantaged. Taking freedoms away never resulted in a gain for the individual, company or society in the long run!

What can be done? It looks like a duality of net technology is in vogue. Simply put, an intranet is installed and dedicated to exclusive internal company working and operations, while an isolated Internet access point is used for everything else. In some cases the intranet becomes a sector wide

Reported (CERT) Internet security incidents

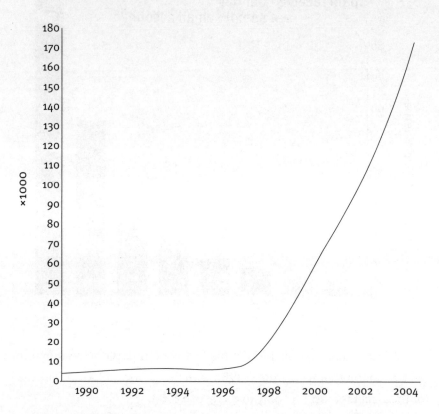

realization, with companies in the same business sharing a common infra-structure.

While I can understand how we got here, I can't say I like the solutions being adopted, as they are tantamount to building separate highways for motorbikes, cars and trucks, bandwidth rich and poor. It doesn't make any economic or operational sense. The real problem is the Internet and WWW have no central authority or organization dedicated to self-defence. In contrast, intranets can be ring-fenced, regulated and controlled to be as safe and secure as reasonably, or unreasonably, possible. And more often than not the practical realization imposes significant limitations on the users!

I would sooner start a war and attack the people responsible by bit and by atom, than see our new freedoms eroded and taken away. A police force with e-SWAT team capabilities is required to take out the various elements dedicated to engineering the economic collapse of individuals, companies, corporations and countries. We certainly should not be rolling over and giving up. In the world of atoms we fight all forms of crime against property, people and companies, so why not in the world of bits?

How could we do it? The first step ought to be the galvanizing of all the ISPs to be responsible in the provision of service and the guarding of information highways and bit transfers. The second step could be the banning of individuals and groups responsible for any criminal activity such as viruses and denial of service attacks. Do it once, get caught, and you are banned for a decade! The third step might be the creation of secure software that makes it very difficult to become a criminal or a victim. Guardians, gatekeepers, identifiers, encryption, reverse virus and worm technologies are all available or feasible but not implemented, to date.

It has always seemed strange that the police forces and legal systems of the planet can cope with car crime, burglary, assault, fraud and all things physical but relatively speaking have no facility for or jurisdiction over the eWorld. Why are we not tracking down the criminals responsible for viral attacks? We should also track down those who deny companies service by flooding servers with unwanted messages? Why is there no specific criminal code applicable to the WWW? I think the answer to all this is obvious and it is clear it will be a very long time before we get an Internet police force.

In previous eras of human history the wild and lawless have reigned for some time before being overcome by those focused on doing good. Vigilantes and kangaroo courts usually preceded the rule of law and order, with transitions that have been bloody and violent. It might just be that we are about to see history repeated yet again on another frontier using slightly different techniques!

If we do nothing we will see one of the most successful communication technologies we ever invented and deployed consigned to history, or at least the shadows, within five years. The corporate control freaks will fill the vacuum and our global freedom will be significantly impaired. I'm afraid the clock is ticking.

Byte 36
Who'd Be a Copyright Lawyer?

Imagine, just a few years from now, being able to store every film and song ever released on a single device. Now imagine content companies that can't come around to embracing that.

Having successfully killed Napster the attention of the music industry has turned to peer-to-peer networking, ISPs and box shifters. Yes, PCs, cameras, hi-fis, PDAs, in fact every conceivable hardware box, past, present and future is coming under the gaze of the copyright soldiers. They are on the warpath, on a mission to constrict and constrain human creativity, and marshalling political resources to take on all potential violators with their outdated laws.

Producers of PCs, DVD players and hi-fis are being pressured by the music and movie industries to build in hardware and software disablers to prevent copying. This is control freakery on steroids! Don't they get it? This is hopeless and futile?

I am writing this on the Ipswich to London train. Opposite me are a couple of youngsters operating laptop computers back to back. What are they doing? Swapping huge music files. This is pure, unstoppable P2P. Who needs the net?

In the same way, software viruses only need four or five hops to infect every computer on the planet, the same is true of music tracks. Or those worth listening to, at least. When these youngsters alight the train they will pass on their new gains to other friends, and inside a week the music will be around the planet. P2P is not just across a table or room, it is planet wide. Can it be stopped? Not a chance.

Balance of income on intellectual property

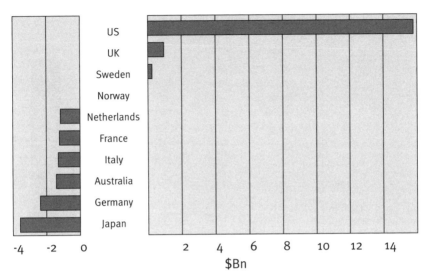

$Bn

Will the music, movie and book publishers and their lawyers continue their futile crusade? Oh yes! But at every turn they will be outmanoeuvred and confounded by millions realizing their freedom of choice. They can select their individual choice of track, clip and page, and no longer have to buy unwanted material in huge quantities. No matter what hardware or software fixes they come up with, a workaround will be on the market within days and their control standards will be systematically usurped.

Do I believe in copyright? No, but I do believe in paying, and people receiving just reward for their work. Producers need rewarding or ultimately there will be no material to copy. What is fundamentally wrong is the current industry model. Copyright restrictions are out of touch with modern society, technology and needs. A new commercial model affording a far greater latitude is required to offset uncontrolled and illegal copying.

The entertainment industries initially fought audio and videotape, and indeed the CD to the death, but each technology has brought them great wealth. They are now trying to cripple and prevent direct copying but they will fail here too. The flawed logic is being applied to the net for the same misguided reasons, it is all about control. They argue that the artists and writers are being ripped off, but the bloated music and publishing industries

Growth of information

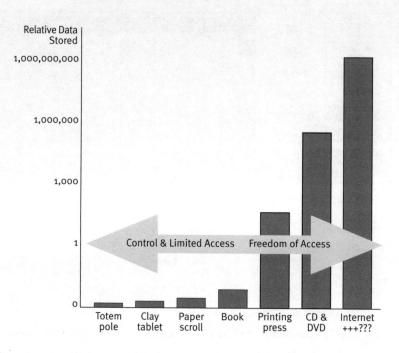

Relative Data Stored

1,000,000,000

1,000,000

1,000

1

0

Control & Limited Access → Freedom of Access

Totem pole | Clay tablet | Paper scroll | Book | Printing press | CD & DVD | Internet +++???

have been ripping them off for decades. A CD complete with plastic box and cover costs less than $1 to manufacture and deliver to the shops, but we all pay $20, and the artist will be lucky to get $1 in royalties.

The incorrect thinking of industry is that all those P2P transactions can be translated directly into $$$ sales. This simply isn't going to happen. I am 57 years old and still have a conscience. I still pay for my books, music and videos. However, once those bits are mine they get ripped, stripped and stored on multiple hard drives that I own. Bluntly, I object to buying a music CD full of crap just to get at the two tracks I really want; but I pay, take the tracks that I want and dispose of the rest – the atoms – the discs go straight in the trash. I can't afford the physical storage space and I don't like the clutter. The important fact is this: young people don't give a second thought to going well beyond this. They don't care if what they do is declared illegal – it makes sense – uncommon sense!

The new consumer has the ability to inflict huge damage on any industry foolish enough to launch products such as content-controlled CDs or regionally limited DVDs. No matter what an industry does there will be workarounds. Encrypt or disable tracks to prevent direct copying and somewhere there is a kid smart enough to screw the system and find a solution.

So what can be done? Industry needs to think through its business model, to recognize disruptive technology is often fatal to those who do not adapt. They will have to sell bits direct, they will have to reward artists and writers more effectively, and they will have to give customers what they want. Music tracks at $1 a time on the net will sell but not at $20 on a CD! Moreover, those who think that downloads principally get burnt onto CDs are wrong – they go onto hard drives, multiple hard drives. The clock is definitely ticking.

Finally, for the industry and its lawyers I would like to post a warning: it really is going to get much worse. Within a decade computers will have clock speeds 1000 times faster than today, and holographic DVDs (for want of a better name) will have a storage capacity far in excess of 1,000,000Gbytes. I predict we are close to getting enough capacity to store every movie and music track ever recorded on a single device. Ouch! I wouldn't be a copyright lawyer for anything. It may be time to move on!

Software Licensing – Time To Get Angry

Licensed? Incensed, more like. Current licensing, which just has to change ...

When I first started in personal computing most software came on floppy disks, was intuitive, fast to load and simple to operate. It never seemed to come with handbooks, terms and conditions or, indeed, a licence. Today software arrives on CD or DVD or is downloaded over the Internet and is far more complex, with handbooks and lots of incomprehensible documentation. Most prominent in all of this is the now ubiquitous software licence.

For many years I would load software, read the gradually growing tomes of documentation that ultimately included copyright, terms and conditions of use, and licence. I would agree to all these and activate the content to get full use. Gradually I began to lapse into a default state of acceptance without reading.

This situation ensued for years until recently, when I took to reading through the now very long licence conditions associated with all my software purchases. Bluntly, I have become alarmed at what I have been agreeing to in the past and what I am expected to sign up to today. Licences often state that I agree to the supplier having the right to modify its software, and indeed other software content, on my machine at some future date.

I wonder how many of you have read a software licence and, if you have, rejected the application on the basis of handing over control to the supplier? Not many, I fancy. Suddenly we are faced with a dangerous situation where the control of our machines is gradually being handed over to a few giant corporations, by default. I for one have started to avoid agreeing to all forms of software licence or accepting terms and conditions that hand

Typical software license agreement

- By using the software (whether you have registered the software or not), you are agreeing to be bound by these terms.

So why bother reading or agreeing – I'm dead in the water no matter what!

- If you do not agree to the terms of this agreement, do not use the software and destroy all copies in your possession.

What – after spending $87?

- The software is owned by *Company X* protected by US copyright and you must treat the software like any book or musical recording.

I might lend a friend a book or a CD, and more than one person can listen to it at a time.

- This license does not allow the software to exist on more than one computer – you may make one copy for backup only.

As I have three computers on my network this is very inconvenient and/or expensive.

- If you violate any part of this agreement, your right to use this software terminates automatically and you must then destroy all copies of the software in your possession.

Wishful thinking!

- We do not warrant that the functions in the software will meet your requirements or that the operation will be error free.

Fancy buying a car or TV on this basis?

- Under no circumstances shall *Company X* be liable for any incidental, special, or consequential damages that result from the use or inablility to use the software or related documentation.

The software company takes no responsibility at all?

- Agreement shall be governed by the laws of the state of California.

In China? I don't think so!

over control of my future. I have started to freeze some software upgrades and new applications on the basis of future risk.

Recently I was involved in a comprehensive discussion on this issue with large corporate software users and was surprised to find that several had frozen their IT progress at the year 1998 or 2000. What's more, these corporates were refusing to upgrade any software from now on. They had stockpiled applications, licences and tools that they felt would be sufficient to see them through the next decade without the need to upgrade. In their words: *'Why would we upgrade anything at great expense and huge risk of external control when we see no advantage in the new products on offer?'*

There seems to be a mindset that has spread from controlling content, in terms of the printed word, graphics, movies and music, through to computer operating systems and software applications. It began with the copyright and protection and then moved on to control.

Along with many others I was bemused by the music industry destroying Napster and the MP3 wars that followed. This has included the arrival of content-controlled CDs and more recently the attempts to make it legal to attack peer-to-peer software and networks. I have also witnessed young people, frustrated by these intrusions, bypass all attempts at software and network control. This has included legal, semi-legal and wholly illegal (by today's definitions and standards) actions on the part of the invisible community of incensed users.

In the parallel universe of the PC I now find an increasing number of Web sites where you can download complete software applications that have been stripped from their original source. These are devoid of control, licence, or payment, and are entirely illegal, breaching all copyright and reasonable licence terms and conditions. Of course this has all been prompted by software producers trying to assume control of their customers. I think we will have to call this Copyright Wars – and I only see a really bad ending to the whole game. Industry and users will both lose.

In areas of Southeast Asia it is possible to buy CDs for $1, no matter what the content. Your choice of music, graphics, movie, applications and operating system – it doesn't matter – everything is just $1. For the most part it seems that all license information has been deleted, or worked around, and copyright is ignored or goes unapplied. Now this is really dangerous and way beyond the CD/DVD rippers and strippers in the West, and I can only imagine the $Bns that must be lost to the authors and producers.

It is hard to find an upside to all this, but a new industry has been born out of the frustration created by those seeking to control every bit on the planet. Thousands of individuals now create an unlimited and unbounded supply of applications and materials made available free or at a very modest fee. The largest of these is the Linux operating system that has been written and supplied on a free basis for almost all hardware platforms.

The mighty software industry may be powerful and clever but what they are up against is millions of bright people who are determined to maintain their freedom. I think what is required here is an injection of sanity. On every occasion in the past, when some force or power has tried to fetter and control the human mind, spirit and progress, they have ultimately failed. Whether a financial or a political system, it is immaterial. People cherish their freedom above all and will commit what is considered to be a crime today to achieve a free world tomorrow. Ultimately I can only see a lot of pain for providers who continue trying to control the machines, minds and pockets of their customers.

I suspect that a supermarket mentality is at work here. Price the product too high and it won't sell. Price the product too low and it won't sell. Give it away and people won't value it. Get the price, packaging, and positioning just right and you will have a winner. This is all about elasticity – price and perception elasticity, and it isn't a science, it is more of an art or a gamble! But, for sure, a new business model and legal system change is overdue – problem is I don't see anyone addressing the issues – they are just fighting to maintain the status quo.

Technology Fatigue

> *A mobile phone needs a manual in the way that a teacup doesn't.*
>
> Douglas Adams

Technology is advancing so fast, but we still don't have the simple things we want. Will the industry ever learn?

Over the past three years everyone seems to have developed technology fatigue, with most overwhelmed by the fire hose of new products announced by the day. People can't decide whether to buy or wait a few weeks and get a much better model at a lower price. At the same time we are prone to worry about being able to understand and adapt to the myriad of new features that follow model on model. And then there is *feature death* – will it all work and live up to the vision of simplicity, reward and satisfaction the advertisers and promoters sell to us?

I think we have entered an IT era where almost everything is beginning to look stale. Each laptop looks more flash than the previous one, with improvements that are largely aesthetic, while the fundamental capability is more of the same, only faster. The software and applications are familiar but more complex – and *feature death* has become a plague.

I can remember when it was possible to know all of the intimate corners of a word processor, graphics package or mobile phone application. But no longer! It is impossible to navigate all the features without the use of obscenely large handbooks and complicated procedures that often defy the dexterity of my fingers and visual resolution.

It seems to me that we are rapidly heading to a 'Moore's Wall' of creativity and interface. There is absolutely no slowdown in signal-processing

More and more powerful mobile devices in shorter and shorter times...

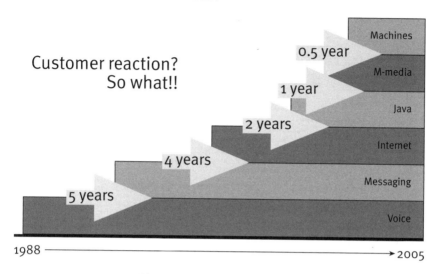

Customer reaction?
So what!!

0.5 year
1 year
2 years
4 years
5 years

Machines
M-media
Java
Internet
Messaging
Voice

1988 —————————————————————→ 2005

More:
Mobile than fixed
Messages than voice
Net purchases than a PC

power, storage capability, display technology and software advancement. Nor is there any slowdown in our ability to create fixed and mobile bandwidth for connectivity. But our interface innovation is moving at a crawl!

What is happening may be a consequence of mistiming. The sluggish rollout of broadband contributed to the dot-com crash and the hype of a digital world raised and then dashed people's expectations to the point where the majority are largely disinterested. Worse, most major players have slashed R&D budgets and focused their attention on milking the assets.

Is it any surprise that some countries are seeing the demand for broadband tailing off early? People have had to make do and make mend, and have got by with peer-to-peer (P2P) networking. And where is the content? Where are the big life-changing gains? Individuals and companies have been screaming for bandwidth for years, and now broadband delivers so little! Why the surprise when people try the net once and never return or refuse to buy a new mobile phone when the prices have been doubled to subsidize the 3G fiasco? It should now be all about content, services and value.

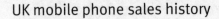

UK mobile phone sales history

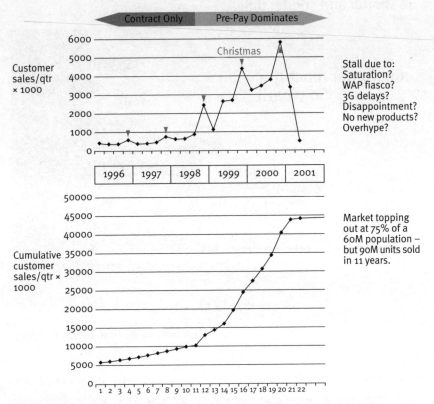

The IT industry's biggest problem is deciding what and when people will purchase, and then supplying it just in time. If you over/under provide/deliver/sell, or mistime, the result is punishing – a downturn in demand of the form we are now witnessing.

Certainly the base technologies have not under-delivered, but promises have been made that haven't been fulfilled and customers are disappointed with WAP, GPRS, Bluetooth and broadband. TV and movie adverts showing people surfing the Web on a mobile phone or watching a movie are a long way from reality and as soon as customers discover this, their reaction is rapid and one-way.

Can the industry get out of this hole? I think so, but it will take a co-ordinated and phased activity that sees bandwidth to the home, office and mobile device universally available. Alongside this we'll need devices that can exploit this bandwidth and provide recognizable services and value to customers. The really bad news is that customers are not going to pay. The old notion that you charge by the bit, minute and mile is long dead, along with the fallacy that disposable income per head can magically and instantaneously grow to fill the coffers of the provisioning companies.

There is now an expectation that the processing power and storage capability of devices will double each year and the price will remain the same or drop a little. That expectation is being passed into the world of networks, and the biggest growth area that none of them are able to access and extract value from is P2P networking. What has happened right under their nose is the creation of a new mobile network born of consumer frustration with the lack of networked bandwidth. It is not by accident that bigger hard drives and portable storage devices are selling so well!

P2P is now responsible for moving more MBytes of entertainment data than all the optical fibre and wireless systems combined. Increasingly, people are moving files of huge dimensions from one device to another at close quarters and then physically carrying them across the planet to a location and sharing them. Sure, this is a slow network, but the bandwidth is enormous and the cost to the participants virtually zero <$1/GByte.

All my life working in the industry I listened to people asking a fundamental question – why do people want all this bandwidth and what will they do with it? And I keep uttering the same response – it's none of our damn business. When you go to buy a car the salesman doesn't ask you what you are going to use it for and he certainly doesn't try to persuade you to buy a bicycle instead. He is very happy for you to trade-up and spend more money, irrespective of what you want to buy. Until the networking companies adopt the same attitude, we are going to see a growing glitch in the sale of technology and the satisfaction of customer demands.

Byte 39
Circuit or Packet – Clean or Dirty?

For many people the quality of the speech and the vision provided by IP technology is adequate, but for professional use it will never make the grade on today's Internet.

Will the telephone network be wiped out by the Internet? Will Voice Over Internet Protocol (VOIP) win the battle? Will Video Conferencing Over Internet Protocol (VCOIP) become a mass market? My opinion is: *YES, it will happen eventually*, but not overnight. The principal reason for my assessment is a simple one. The bandwidth dedicated to the voice and video traffic of the telephone network is currently far in excess of that used for the Internet. There just isn't a one-to-one mapping between the old circuit-switched and new packet-switched networks – yet!

The predominant mode for all real-time human telecommunication is circuit switching, with a dedicated connection between two terminals/ people for their sole use throughout the session. When you pick up a telephone and dial a number, a circuit is established between you and whoever you call, which lasts for the duration of your conversation. The same is true for video conferencing and all real-time services.

For non real-time applications such as email, messaging, computer communications, and delayed voice and video we can use packet switching, where the digital information is broken up into small packets and directed one at a time (or in groups) across the planet, using any available routing at the time of despatch. Instead of a known and dedicated connection, each packet may arrive by vastly different routings (and therefore transmission delays) to be reassembled in the correct order at the reception point.

The circuit and packet-switched (IP – VOIP) space

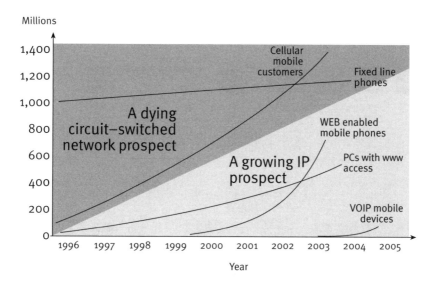

This subtle difference between circuit and packet switching was established by technologies of two different eras. When the telephone system was first implemented the electronics to do anything sophisticated were just not available. At this time the thermionic tube (the valve) had not been invented and everything was electro-mechanical. Moreover, dedicated circuits between customers had to be established through multiple (concatenated) switching sites and routings to establish a continuous communication path.

It was the need for computer communication that created the packet-switched philosophy, to obviate the need for 100% dedicated circuits and increase communication efficiency. At that time such connections were very expensive, and computers inherently need to communicate with multiple destinations at the same time for seconds rather than point to point for minutes. Today we communicate at will from any location and at any time, but most have absolutely no idea how the circuits are configured or how they operate, and why should they? But, if you stop for a moment and wonder how you would engineer a system that would allow any two people out of a 1,000,000,000 population, distributed over 200 countries, to connect and speak at will … this is not a trivial problem!

Circuit and packet-switched networks

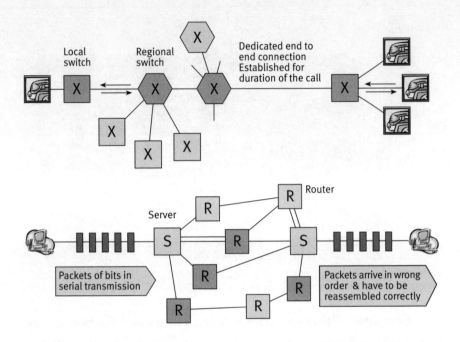

The actual solution is currently in a critical cost and performance battle between two distinct philosophies – circuit and packet switching. In most towns you will find a telephone exchange that occupies several floors of a large building, in that same town you will find an ISP, providing a packet-switching capability in a single room, or indeed a single equipment cabinet. As the bits per second passing through these facilities are roughly of the same order of magnitude, the promise is that huge (and very expensive) circuit switches (occupying buildings) could be replaced by something that is far less expensive that would easily fit into your garage.

If you ever have the chance to experience a VOIP telephone call or VCOIP, take advantage of the experience and watch and listen for the artefacts. It is impossible to control the Internet in the same way we control the telephone network, and so congestion, collisions and traffic jams cause delays and bunching of packets in an unpredictable manner. A huge amount of effort had been expended trying to cure or, better, circumvent this problem. The most successful attempts see the prescriptive routing and priority of packets so the end-to-end circuit, although based on packets, rapidly resembles its circuit-switched predecessor. For many people the quality of the speech and the vision provided by IP technology is adequate, but for professional use it will never make the grade in any ubiquitous sense, and there is now an invisible and unvoiced movement to create a second, very clean and controlled, Internet.

It has been widely proven that VOIP and VCOIP can be engineered over private intranets, where the bandwidth and the collisions (traffic jams) can be controlled. So many companies are having their circuit-switched private networks (PBX) replaced by IP-based networks (intranets) on which computers and people can communicate. One of the secrets for success is an overall reduction in the number of hops and switching/routing nodes from one point to another and the strict control of the traffic to give priority to all real-time applications.

It is clear that the global telephone network cannot be wholly replaced by the uncontrolled and chaotic Internet without drastic modification and investment. But the joining together of purpose-engineered intranets could edge us slowly towards a world where no one produces a circuit-switch machine ever again. The reality is that no one has a tried and tested model that allows us to engineer this today, but there are some very strong contenders. Industry faces an interesting predicament, where no one is willing to manufacture big telephone switches any more, and no one quite knows how to replace them with the packet-switch equivalent. In the meantime the old switches are getting even older and not being replaced. So the clock is definitely ticking for an industry born of the 19th century!

I think we are about to see the emergence of a new and clean Internet, one that is controlled and not subject to hacker attack or subversive use, but maintained by companies and organizations for the express purpose of driving down the cost of telephone and video communication and providing a greater utility than is available hitherto. The IP takeover is well underway, and in the USA companies increasingly offer me a 'dirty Internet' connection as a visitor, whilst employees enjoy a 'clean Internet' facility that has replaced the 'dirty Internet' and PBX. *For IP it is not a question of 'if', but 'when'.*

Byte 40
It's Our Brains That Lack Bandwidth

Why do telcos baby their customers – could it be they're waiting for us to catch up with the technology?

Throughout my 40+ years in the telecom industry there have been interminable discussions and debate on bandwidth demand. In the 1960s it was: 'How could we possibly use 2Mbit/s to the business, let alone the home?' (Such a bit transfer rate would see an average paperback novel transmitted across the planet in slightly over 1 second, 32 simultaneous telephone conversations, and TV pictures poorer than VHS and broadcast quality.) Very shortly, demand saw systems migrate to 8Mbit/s, then 32 and 140Mbit/s. Again this was quickly followed by 565Mbit/s, 2400 and then 10,000Mbit/s = 10Gbit/s. Today systems are available at 40Gbit/s and we have 160Gbit/s (and even higher) on the horizon. At each epoch the debate rages – why do people want more and more bandwidth?

So far the demand appears to be insatiable and the industry response inverted and irrational. Suppose, for a moment, a telco was to sell cars. In the showroom they would have something exciting like a BMW 7 series. The salesman would come over. He would be very nice to you and tell you all about the vehicle. He would take you for a drive and convince you it is what you want. However, at the moment of signing the cheque he would stop you and ask a fundamental question: 'What do you want the vehicle for?' Should you reply, 'I will be using it to go to the supermarket on a Friday night to collect my shopping,' he would push you over to the other side of the showroom and insist that you really need the latest Smart Car for a fraction of the price, with of course a fraction of the space and performance.

Worldwide bandwidth demand

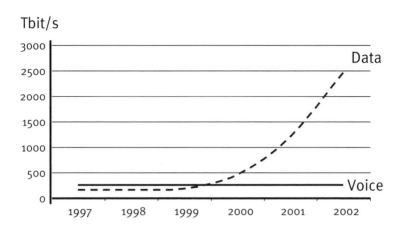

Individual bandwidth demand

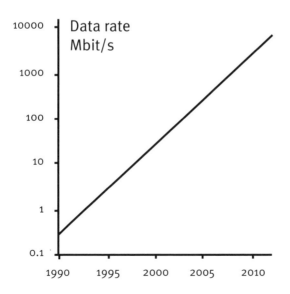

Consumer Internet usage trends

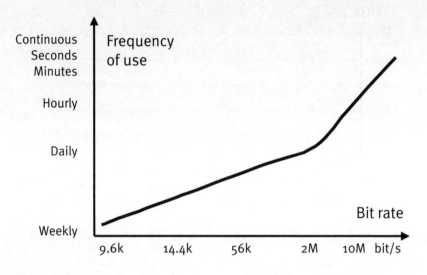

No real car salesman asks you what you want a car for and what you are going to do with it, but the telecoms industry habitually wants to do just that. It really is nothing to do with them – it is time they got out of the customer's space and face. They really do need to take the attitude – if someone asks for 2Mbit/s, you sell it to them. If they want 8Mbit/s you sell it to them. You give them what they want. This is what a real business is supposed to do – JSI (Just Sell/Supply IT).

Of all the things we can manufacture, bandwidth is the cheapest. Our productivity with software is still only around 5% p.a. For hardware it's well over 60%, and bandwidth is in excess of 85%. The cost of bandwidth falls exponentially every year, faster even than RAM, hard drives and clock speed. So why do we hoard it?

To paraphrase George Guilder:

> 'The bandwidth available to the individual will dramatically and continuously increase whilst costs will plummet, and we can expect our individual demands to double every 18 months for at least the next 20 years.'

And the significance of all this? In my view it will be far greater than that of road, rail and air transport combined!

But where does it all go, and why will we need more? There is no doubt about it, our species are great communicators – we love nothing better! I look at it like this: when we communicate we do so through our eyes, ears, skin and olfactory senses, all of which are surface-area related. The flow of information itself is to do with surface area. In contrast our processing of information, our thinking ability and reasoning relates to the volume of our brain, which contains an estimated 10^{10} or so interconnected neurons.

From your high school days, you can probably remember that surface area is related to radius squared and volume is related to radius cubed when we are dealing with a sphere. For the purposes of argument and simplification let's assume the human head and entity is spherical in nature. Given we are extremely head-dominated from an I/O point of view this is not a bad approximation!

So we have information flow going up as r^2 and creativity going up as r^3. As an intellectual exercise you might like to plot those two functions on a piece of paper and you will find that for $r < 1$, $r^3 < r^2$ but once r is > 1, then r^3 increases much faster than r^2 and the two functions have crossed over forever. So for $r > 1$, then $r^3 > r^2$.

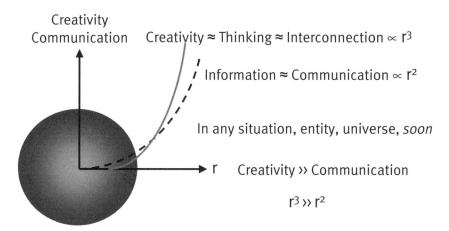

Creativity
Communication

Creativity ≈ Thinking ≈ Interconnection ∝ r^3

Information ≈ Communication ∝ r^2

In any situation, entity, universe, *soon*

Creativity ≫ Communication

$r^3 ≫ r^2$

r

There is never ... enough bandwidth

Why is this important? What can we infer? There comes a point when our communication ability limits our creativity. Our brain needs more I/O – we need to communicate – but we are limited by our sensory system. Our creativity becomes bottled-up and constrained. This applies to all intelligent entities and networks, be they biological, electronic or photonic. When the volumetric thinking capability is far greater then the ability to communicate we hit our fundamental creativity limit or capacity.

If we were to add a few seconds delay to a human conversation it soon becomes stilted and worthless. If we constrain the bandwidth of a speech path, à la the telephone, we remove the emotion, and the value of a conversation is diminished. Our rate of thinking is related to our rate of communication. Slow down communication and you slow down thought and creativity.

Today that is what is happening in industry, education, office and home, and it is beginning to cripple some societies. If you compare different countries and cultures there are clear and remarkable differences in their ability to create wealth and adapt to new technology. But communication is the fundamental component at the heart of all these changes.

Only ten years ago we were waiting for the next slice of technology, as our abilities were clearly limited by technology. Today the converse is true: the technology is waiting for us. Waves of new technology are now arriving faster than we can subsume and adapt and we have become the limiters of progress. Bandwidth is not just the exception; it is a primary cause!

Byte 41

Save Everything – But Don't Be Tidy

> *Man's desires are limited by his perceptions. No one can desire what he has not perceived.*
>
> William Blake

With storage now so cheap should companies even be thinking about deleting old data?

For the first 20 years of my working life I established and took pride in the systematic reading of all relevant reports and publications, their recording, cataloguing and filing. But little by little, the amount of published material increased, as did my span of responsibilities and activities. Things began to slip and accelerate away from me, and gradually I began to get behind with a backlog that started to grow and become beyond my ability and time to recover.

Eventually it became imperative that I develop new strategies to survive the growing tidal wave of information. Reading much faster was the first solution, but that didn't hold back the tide for long. The next was getting others to read for me and provide a verbal brief, but this seemed wasteful and somehow wrong, and so I developed a text-précis software system to take out the people. This too eventually faltered and so my current protocol works as follows:

1   Is the document title interesting and relevant? If NO, then delete or destroy.
2   Are the graphs, pictures and illustrations interesting and relevant? If NO, then delete or destroy.

3   If YES to the above read the abstract. Is it interesting and relevant? If NO, then delete or destroy.
4   If YES to any of the above (1–3) decide to read NOW or LATER.
5   If LATER, enter into electronic or paper read file.
6   After a fast skim read, précis, or detail reading, save electronic copies, or scan-in all paper pages.
7   Extract any illustrations and tables of interest and file.
8   File the electronic copies.
9   Destroy all paper copies.

Now here comes the hard part! I average >1000 documents a year for filing, and I don't have time to be a librarian, to studiously catalogue and file away all this material. Of necessity I had to find an alternative solution, which turned out to be counter intuitive and counter cultural in terms of the corporate tidy minds in industry.

Throughout my life, I have been racked by a need to be tidy and well ordered. My parents, schoolteachers, professors, and mentors in industry impressed the basics upon me – from toys, clothes, tools, books, folders and all work materials – a place for everything and everything in its place! All of my computer desktops and hard drives are well ordered, systematic and sorted. And I similarly started by methodically filing everything scanned into folders, but this quickly degenerated to a uni-heap system. A single folder filing system for all random input seems a bit drastic, but it works. Just throw it all in a pile and use the FIND function when searching seems to do the trick. I have thousands of files accumulated over decades that I never sort, review, check, order, catalogue, or indeed clear out. Provided hard drives continue to get bigger and cheaper, this should be OK for the future too!

I should point out that not all of my filing is done this way. When I create new documents I file them neatly in well-organized folders. And I may be just wasting my time, but I don't have the courage to go the whole hog and move to a single uni-heap system for absolutely everything. I just can't seem to shake off the teachings of my parents, teachers and mentors!

When I compare all this to nature it seems genetics may be the nearest equivalent. Our genome is a library of countless past failures and bad ideas. We all carry the code of the most primitive of animals in our evolutionary record, and we are mostly configured from a lot of old junk no one ever bothered to file correctly or delete. Our basic genetic specification has never been tidied up and over 99% of our genomic data could probably be thrown away and we would be none the worse for the loss. In fact we may well be significantly enhanced and far less susceptible to mutation engendered disease. So why am I worrying about the chaos of my filing system? I'm equally sure 99% of that could be thrown away and I wouldn't even notice.

Whilst the natural world seems fundamentally chaotic there is an interesting meld of order and chaos. Crystals are a primary example with atoms distributed on a regular lattice to create quartz and diamond. The number of petals on a flower also observes a well-ordered pattern. Between the extremes of order and chaos we see widely differing electrical, chemical, mechanical and biological properties. Moreover, our perception and perspectives are also governed by this span. Absolute symmetry of form and architecture are often less interesting and appealing. The inclusion of a few flaws and disorder can be magical in the definition of character and attractiveness.

So does all this translate into our IT-dominated lives and my filing crisis? I think so. Libraries, books and PCs are mostly semi-chaotic filing systems brimming with unwanted junk. We may strive to be tidy and ordered, to dispense with the unwanted and no longer required, but we are not very good at it. The good news is that it doesn't seem to matter, as our storage technology is keeping ahead of our ability to create even more junk.

This is all fortuitous as we lack the means to decide which data to keep or which to destroy. Whilst our photographs, letters, emails and video files may be of interest in 100 years, our tax records can be legitimately destroyed in 7 years. Some companies already destroy all paper correspondence over 12 months old and, in a fast-moving world, could they afford to keep it all anyway?

Global hard drive storage growth

is faster than any other commodity we produce –
and we can assume a near infinite capacity
in future

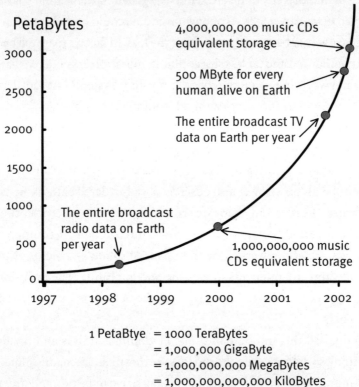

PetaBytes

4,000,000,000 music CDs
equivalent storage

3000

500 MByte for every
human alive on Earth

2500

The entire broadcast TV
data on Earth per year

2000

1500

1000

The entire broadcast
radio data on Earth
per year

500

1,000,000,000 music
CDs equivalent storage

0

1997   1998   1999   2000   2001   2002

1 PetaBtye = 1000 TeraBytes
            = 1,000,000 GigaByte
            = 1,000,000,000 MegaBytes
            = 1,000,000,000,000 KiloBytes
            = 1,000,000,000,000,000 Bytes

I am well aware that passing anything off as useless today will mean that I need it tomorrow! My new IT credo is to just collect and record everything that looks interesting and never throw anything away. I can't afford the time to trawl through all my old records and sort the good from the bad, and with storage space that is so cheap anyway, who cares – I'll just buy another hard drive and file or delete the old one! And with ever faster computing chips and file access times I should be all set to use the Find function to locate anything I need in the future.

Byte 42
The Blue Sack

Read this and see if you still don't care about storage ...

As a child I can remember being fascinated by the late evening ritual of the shops in my small town closing and the proprietors marching down the street, carrying their blue sacks, which would be pushed into a hole in the wall of the bank. For years this mystified me. Then I started to understand the concept of money and the need for banks. What I had seen was the shopkeepers depositing their monies into the wall safe, night on night.

Today that small town has grown dramatically and boasts a large shopping centre. Shopkeepers no longer take part in the daily march down the street to deposit their daily takings. Instead the security companies arrive with their armoured vehicles to collect. Some have a small safe for cash, given that most transactions are now by card or cheque. These businesses now rely on the PC to keep all transaction records and stock control. They have become bit-based rather than atom-based.

What is surprising is that these shopkeepers now close in the evening by switching off a PC and going home. What happens if there is a fire that destroys the shop, or it is burgled and the PC stolen? Most businesses would be wiped out because there would be no easy means of recovery.

The smartest corporations I ever worked with had a daily regime of backing-up individual PCs and workstations, office by office. Each office had a central cache, that in turn backed-up onto a remotely located country server. The best multinationals would also back up each country on at least three continents. Such a daily regime ensures that fire, theft, damage, failure, natural or man-made disasters cannot take down an entire business. It also provides an added degree of resilience against viral and other forms of attack.

Hard drive memory cost

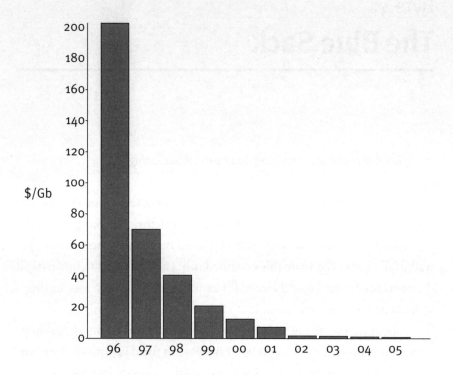

$/Gb

So, the demise of an individual PC, office cache or plant does not disable a complete business. Unfortunately, for many small- to medium-sized enterprises the culture of backup and security is not ubiquitous. Many are therefore at considerable risk from a number of directions.

In my own case, which involves a good deal of travel, losing my laptop would mean the loss of my entire business. So my precautionary regime involves backing-up everything on portable hard drive that mirrors my laptop, but resides in my travel bag, a server in my office, a server in my secretary's home and burning a hard copy onto CDs deposited in my daughter's home. The three buildings involved are geographically dispersed and the likelihood of a simultaneous disaster or hit is extremely remote, and more especially so when I am also on the road.

On a personal level there is now another dimension to the loss of business data and the loss of business as a result – the loss of critical personal possessions. If you talk to people who have suffered a house fire, burglary,

The future of individual storage

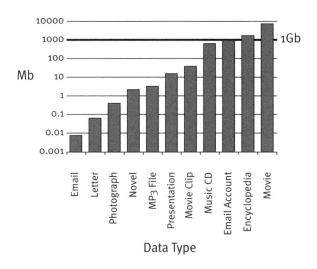

Data Type

flooding or some other natural disaster that has taken away all their possessions, what they really mourn is not those pieces of furniture or expensive consumer gadgets, but personal items such as jewellery and heirlooms. Family photographs in particular are prized by all of us and yet are so easily lost.

The first time I realized that I should do something about the family photograph collection was when I noticed some chemical deterioration of prints going back 100 years. I was quite alarmed at the rate at which this was progressing. So my youngest son helped scan in all of the photographs from all parts of the family and commit them to CD and hard drives. I now feel reasonably content that any natural disaster, fire, theft or other action will not deprive my future family of the recorded past.

Over a year ago now, the same son persuaded me to build a large server for our home of a far greater capacity than I thought we would ever need – 1000GByte (= 1TByte). Just 12 months later it is getting full. It contains business records alongside a vast photographic past of family through several generations. It is also starting to accumulate a library of movie clips, professional presentations, music and media of all kinds. My problem now is how to back this up.

Even during the construction of this mighty beast, one hard drive mechanically failed and the read-write arm descended into the disc at full speed, totally destroying the content. Fortunately I had taken the precaution of having duplicate hard drives on the server. What business, families and individuals will ultimately require is network caching on which to duplicate everything. Network-based storage is going to be big business in the future and the ultimate mechanism for ensuring we don't lose our heritage or our business.

I am pleased to say that as I write the cost of hard drives has fallen to < $1/GByte, and commercial 500GByte (FireWire) units are on the market for just $750. So it would appear we are on the verge of a new market – the home and office server of near infinite capacity. It can only get better!

Some years ago the city of Norwich saw its medieval Central Library destroyed by fire. In one conflagration its valuable records were lost forever. Prior to this, and similar losses, people decried computer technology and the committing of ancient documents to bits rather than atoms. Even today I hear people argue that data storage is volatile and dangerous and everything should be retained on paper, parchment and velum. Yet, after a series of fires throughout Europe that have destroyed a great deal of heritage, people are gradually recognizing that bit storage over a number of dispersed locations is the only sure way we can establish any guarantee of longevity. Laboriously scanning in documents, sheet by sheet, may seem expensive until that information is lost forever, and for business it can be the end of the line!

Byte 43
Being a Squirrel

What value has all that information accrued over the years – all those emails, documents, lists and programs?

After 38 years in my previous company, I left with a large collection of boxes containing artefacts of all kinds, reflecting a lifetime's scientific and engineering effort. Over a year later a large number of these boxes were still in my garage, and I was still systematically sorting through them and throwing away things I could part with and mothballing things I couldn't.

Probably one of the most surprising outcomes from this archaeological dig was the amount of software on floppy disks and CDs that I had accumulated. I was tempted to destroy the entire collection out of hand, on the basis that I just don't have the time to trawl through for any interesting gems hidden among the mass of detritus. But looking at this pile, I had to relent.

The first surprise was that I no longer have a floppy drive to read most of the material with so I had to search out an old piece of technology to gain access. I then employed my son to transfer the materials from floppy to hard drive so we could access and sort far more rapidly. All the floppy discs were then trashed using a hammer! A bit crude you might think, and I did feel a twinge of guilt being so destructive, but this is the only way you can be 100% sure that the will never be accessed by another hand at some time in the future.

During the protracted scanning exercise came shrieks of delight as my son discovered software older then he was. Further, some applications he currently uses were actually present in their original Version 1.00 form. For example, Microsoft Word and Excel were each contained on a single floppy disk, whilst PowerPoint was found to require less than a single disc. To my amazement all three applications booted-up first time and operated

Changing global storage needs

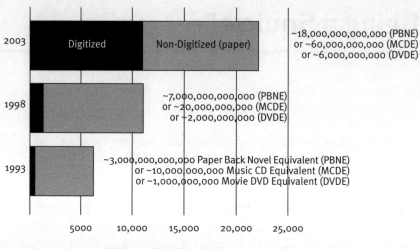

2003 — Digitized | Non-Digitized (paper) — ~18,000,000,000,000 (PBNE) or ~60,000,000,000 (MCDE) or ~6,000,000,000 (DVDE)

1998 — ~7,000,000,000,000 (PBNE) or ~20,000,000,000 (MCDE) or ~2,000,000,000 (DVDE)

1993 — ~3,000,000,000,000 Paper Back Novel Equivalent (PBNE) or ~10,000,000,000 Music CD Equivalent (MCDE) or ~1,000,000,000 Movie DVD Equivalent (DVDE)

5000   10,000   15,000   20,000   25,000

PBytes – all media estimate

1 Petabyte = 1000 Terabytes = 1,000,000 Gigabytes = 1,000,000,000 Megabytes

Historical information growth

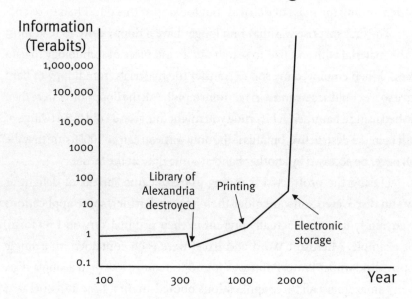

Information (Terabits)

1,000,000
100,000
10,000
1000
100 — Library of Alexandria destroyed — Printing
10
1 — Electronic storage
0.1

100   300   1000   2000   Year

How many American shoes?

- Life expectancy – 77 years

- According to the AAFA, the average American buys 6 pairs of shoes per year = 462 pairs in a lifetime!

Based on a pair of shoes taking up a shelf space of 0.35 m × 0.25 m × 0.15 m

Your shoe rack would look like this:

11.55 m

Americans also average 54 items of clothing/year. A lifetime would require 80 m of storage – the width of a soccer field!

Internet global growth

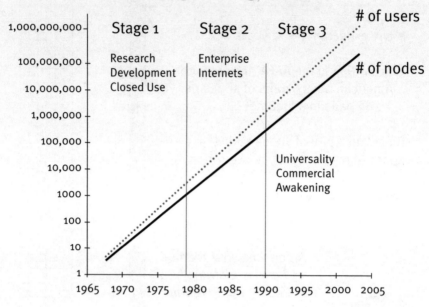

Supporting technology trends

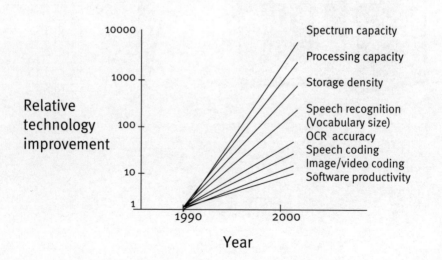

perfectly. Moreover, they looked exactly as they do today, but worked far faster. However, they had thousands of features missing! Alongside these well-known applications were many others I'd not seen for years. Amazingly they all worked right first time! Given the volatility of floppy discs and the decade or more some of these had been stored this seemed to go against all the established wisdoms and factual evidence on long-term storage, which would predict a certainty of data corruption

As we got into the documents, it became increasingly difficult to open files. The further back in time we went the worse it got. Many of the applications seem to have long gone, some were unidentifiable and an extensive amount of detective work was necessary to dig down and eventually open every one. This prompted me to create a museum of software applications on all my machines. A small space on each of my hard drives now contains applications consigned to history and forgotten by many people routinely using computers, never heard of by the vast majority.

I suspect that in the not-too-distant future the need to open old files will be on a par with our current need to be able to read manuscripts from ancient civilizations. Buried in these files among the majority of the information – which is probably worthless – will be gems we should keep for historical and cultural reasons. What is trash today may be valuable tomorrow – and we don't have to actually delete anything anyway – we increasingly have infinite storage.

The second phase of this exercise was to pull out documents from the past, clean them up and save them in a modern and more universal format. The biggest threat to their survival is actually the rapid demise of the operating systems supporting the old applications along with the hardware platforms to run the software.

To say the least this all turned out to be rewarding and a reminder of just how long it takes R&D to make it to the market place. Among the many gems, which I had largely forgotten, was optical fibre with intelligence, where signal processing by photons instead of electrons could be contained in a length of stranded glass. Almost within a week, and out of the blue, I coincidentally received a project proposal from a company embarking on the commercialization of such a technology. Their documentation was full of comments and focus on the new and novel nature of their ideas – which turn out, by my record at least, to be over 15 years old!

The speed-up of technology and the rapid change within companies has seen the accelerating death of the corporate memory. Organizations can no longer remember what was done 5 years ago, let alone 15 years ago, and as our IT accelerates the process even further, this has to be some cause for concern. Perhaps we should contemplate caching all our documents from all companies so we can search by word, topic, date and people to ensure that human effort is not squandered at an increasing rate.

After several days of effort, my son and I had recovered 38 years of my past eLife and reduced it all to a small number of files. Many of these may not be of any direct application in my present or future life, but as an historical record they at least make interesting reading – to me at any rate! And just like my lecture notes from college and university I just cannot bring myself to delete them – I think the sentimental value outweighs the true value by several points.

I can see an end point coming where every hard drive on the planet becomes Napsterized so we may make available complete works and thoughts to a much broader audience than just ourselves. I would like to make a percentage of every hard drive I own available to the rest of humanity and I would like them to reciprocate. It will be the sharing of data, information and experience/s across all countries and cultures that may see our biggest advances as a species. But, it is going to be the categorization, cataloguing, display, searching and finding that is going to be the biggest challenge.

While the Napster model for music created tremendous legal problems, and entertainment/copyright wars that are ongoing and only seem to get worse by the year, I think it really opened the door to a new paradigm that automatically guards against the widespread loss of information, individual, corporate and government memory in the future.

Byte 44
Reliability and Downtime

A 99.999% availability is not easily achieved in complex machines and networks, and it presents a substantial challenge.

The concept of downtime has been with us for around a hundred years and emerged from the early telegraph and telephone network era of two centuries ago. As soon as we moved into telecommunication and extended our reach and control, reliability and availability became an ever-important feature of government, management and society.

Well into the era of the automated telephone, a magic performance figure emerged as a design target for each individual telephone exchange or switch. This was necessary as telephone networks grew across continents and ultimately linked to every nation on the planet – which, by the way, only occurred in my lifetime. The increasing number of concatenated switches and amplifiers for long-distance communications demanded extremely high levels of reliability; the failure of one meant the failure of all. This is the weakest link in the chain problem.

There is now a celebrated figure of five nines often quoted in the industry, which says that a switch has to have an availability (or an uptime in modern parlance) of 99.999% i.e. a probability of 0.99999. That is, in any one year of operation the total unavailability or downtime of a single switch has to be less than 0.0001%, or a probability of 0.00001. This allows a total of only 5.3 minutes in a year.

As an engineer I can tell you that 99.999% is not easily achieved in complex machines and presents a substantial challenge. It dictates the use of multiple battery power supplies, generally backed-up by diesel generators, with many items of the control and switch-gear at least duplicated by hot-

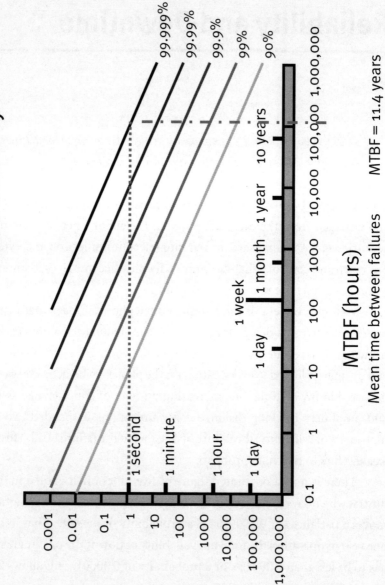

Hot standby and common mode failure

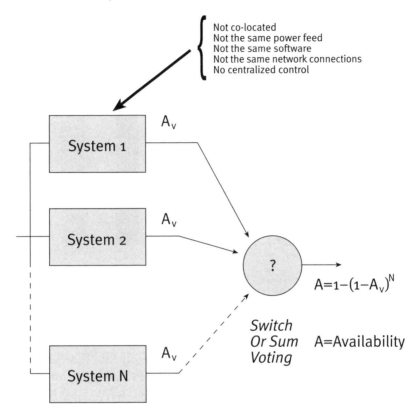

Not co-located
Not the same power feed
Not the same software
Not the same network connections
No centralized control

System 1 A_v

System 2 A_v

System N A_v

?

$A=1-(1-A_v)^N$

*Switch
Or Sum*   A=Availability
Voting

standby circuits. Should any single component fail, all have to be switched over automatically in a seamless manner undetected by the customer.

There are not many items of technology that can boast such a perform-ance, or indeed such a high reliability figure. But when you consider the concatenation of around five switches for a single in-country connection, or ten for an international call, it becomes obvious why this is so necessary. The downtime for 5 concatenated switches increases to around 26 minutes a year, whilst 10 switches will see around 53 minutes a year. This is all still pretty im-pressive, but barely adequate for some modern business, especially banking.

The number of customers served by each switch compounds all of these reliability figures. For example, with 100,000 customers terminated on one switch we have the potential for $100{,}000 \times 5.3$ minutes (~1 year) of total customer downtime!

N + 1 Standby for a single 90% availability units

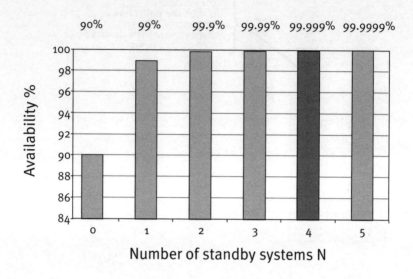

The computer industry looks on 99.999% with some envy and often struggles to approach 99%. Is your PC up and running for 99% of the time or more? How about your ISP? In my experience ISPs have gone from struggling to attain 90% availability to now achieving 99%. It is not that 99.999% can't be achieved, it's just very tough to engineer as systems become increasingly complex, and it is also very expensive.

Reliability is directly related to technological maturity and, as a general rule, the more we use and engage with a technology, the better we understand it and the more likely we are to achieve high reliability. This is axiomatic in the case of the automobile for example, where over the last 25 years it has gone from being a piece of technology to just a car. Today they always work and very seldom fail; 25 years ago the converse was true.

In my experience when trying to connect to ISPs it is not unusual to hear a line-engaged signal or to get a modem that doesn't respond correctly, or some synchronization failure, not to mention disconnections due to some protocol mangle. The opportunities for ISPs to have a connection failure are compounded by a variety of software and hardware suppliers that have immature technologies. This is in complete contrast to the well-established telephone network.

As I spend a good deal of my life on the move I have adopted strategies to combat the shortfall in performance of today's technology and maintain phone and email communication. I have accounts with five ISPs! Roughly speaking, this gives me a downtime $\sim(0.1)$ EXP5 $= 0.00001$ or a 99.999% uptime. Do I actually achieve this? Well not exactly!

Although my laptop is extremely robust and I carry a full backup hard drive in case of theft or severe damage, there are times when I run out of battery power, encounter a software glitch, or can't get an adequate wireless connection. But I am achieving around 99.99% when I do wish to connect. In any year my enforced downtime is only around one hour. Whilst I suspect this figure will remain a distant dream for single ISPs and most users, it is probably a reasonable target for our new mode of mobile business.

To be offline for a full day is clearly unacceptable for any business, but most can live with an hour!

The proliferation of WLANs and Bluetooth may see new levels of connectivity realized by accident. If all the devices I carry can communicate wirelessly, then I may see a combination of digital mobile phone and WLAN roaming agreements securing 99.99% connections. I only need to access my ISP via any media that happens to be available – I just need my laptop the best viable option available in a given location and go with it!.

Many cities now have entire districts contiguously connected by WiFi. If Bluetooth was also adopted in the same way, the connectivity options will also increase. There is a further opportunity as the same technology is adopted for vehicular use. My laptop talking to a passing taxi, bus or train is not beyond feasibility, and has already been demonstrated.

So it looks as if we may achieve the magic 99.999% by default!

Byte 45
Screen Tests

Something as simple as the size of a user interface governs much of what we can do with computers. I envy the 'tell, find and show' machines used in Star Trek …

At the age of 57 the mobile phone and I are not the best of friends. First, I have very large fingers and as phones have become smaller I am increasingly likely to hit more than one key at a time. Secondly, as I get older, I find it increasingly difficult to read anything on a very small screen without changing my glasses, especially in poor lighting conditions.

I purchased a laptop computer with a 39cm screen and large keyboard to remedy this problem. I habitually type using 18 point so I can read with ease in any environment, and expand on this with triple spacing when in a car or on a train to avoid motion sickness. Interestingly this led to a speed-reading technique that tends to make me look a bit insane! If I stare (unblinking for a long time) at my laptop screen and hold down the scroll key with text at 22 point, triple spaced, I can read a full page in *parallel input mode* in a fraction of the usual *word-by-word* serial norm. Try it – see if it works for you!

Where screens are concerned there will come a point where we move away from the very small to the very large. We will be driven by application and the Captain Kirk Condition – the need to address any machine, any screen at will, and in any location. In *Star Trek,* no one really uses or wears small screens (much); they have moved on. They mostly approach any screen, on any deck of any ship, and boldly ask a computer to tell, find and show. I think a similar regime is about to be engineered for you and me.

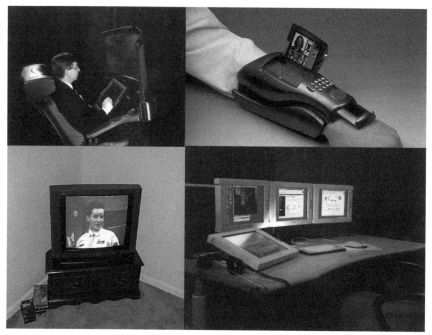

Reproduced by kind permission of BT Laboratories UK

Most mobile phones have a screen measuring a few cm^2 where a limited amount of text and very small pictures can be accommodated. While this may be adequate for telephone calls, text messages, playing very simple computer games and, perhaps, even watching some moving images, it is wholly inadequate for looking at spreadsheets, timetables and most other complex graphical forms. And I am intrigued to see if people will actually stream movies and watch them whilst travelling, as depicted in the TV adverts – but I suspect they will not! The reason? A prohibitive call cost, and an existence theorem that says pocket TV sets are <$100 and have even bigger screens, and fail to sell in large numbers.

Next up the scale is the PDA with a screen area that is roughly ten times bigger than the mobile phone but still less accessible than the laptop computer. Each of these screen formats has yet to find its true place in our IT future.

We now have screens spanning centimetres to metres for mobile and fixed devices. What we don't have are the necessary interfaces to make accessing information intuitively simple. In my ideal world a very large plasma

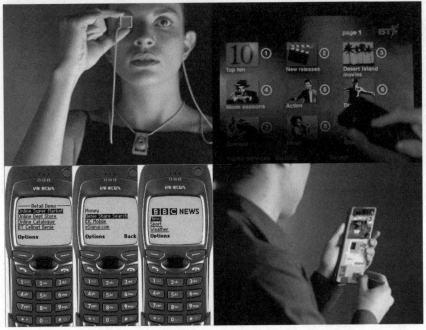

Reproduced by kind permission of BT Laboratories UK

or LCD screen located in any shopping mall, railway station or airport would have a telephone number across the bottom. My mobile phone would be the entry device, I would be able to dial into that screen and talk to the computer using natural spoken language – and keys. And the payment mechanism? Just add it all to my phone bill, please!

I would like to be able to call up any form of information or interaction that is inaccessible on the phone itself. Such a regime has several advantages that those in the business will immediately recognize. For companies installing kiosks in public places it is frustrating to see the occupancy largely dominated by non-customers, people who don't really use them for the purpose they're intended. This includes those who just want to play and those intent on vandalism. Having to use your mobile phone to pay for access would switch off idle curiosity and vandals would have to be incredibly stupid to smash up their own handsets! It would also be almost impossible to damage a plasma/LCD screen behind bulletproof glass.

The benefits could be huge. Those carrying mobile phones would have instant access to information on a screen that would be easily read and far more powerful than a mobile or PDA alone. Suddenly the mobile phone would become the passport to the information world at large and not be limited to today's keyhole view.

The biggest hurdle is the voice interface. There has been little real progress in this arena over the last decade. Silicon speech recognizers have been more efficient than humans on individual words for a long time. The problem is not speech recognition per se but the contextualization and cognition capacities of machines. Without such an ability it may prove impossible for us to ever command, let alone converse, with any machine in a noisy (street, station, airport, mall) environment.

Natural conversation between human and machine, as famously depicted in the movie *2001*, is still a long way off. We have speech synthesis and recognition that is adequate for command and control in reasonably controlled environments and modes. But today's technology is wholly inadequate for a conversational enquiry as demonstrated by Captain Kirk. And the biggest hurdle to this particular Holy Grail? Our inability to fully understand intelligence and cognitive systems in both the carbon and silicon life forms. This seems to be the next big challenge! In the meantime we may have to make do with an environment that assumes our mobile phone is a mouse, and we will just have to continue with the point and click of today – for a while at least.

Byte 46
G-Force

Ever slam down a handset, sit on a mobile phone or dent a laptop?
These days the odds are they'll continue to function.

The escalator down to the baggage claim area at Miami airport is very steep and long. Today I get to the top of it after two weeks of continual travel and in a slightly dazed state, somehow manage to unclip my mobile phone from my belt and it flies down the escalator, bouncing three times. At the bottom there is a pilot and I shout a warning: 'Mobile phone on the way down!' He is obviously a football player as he instinctively turns and traps my phone with his foot in one smooth action. Terrific, no one got hurt.

I'm pretty sure this is the end of my mobile communication for the trip. With some gratitude I accept my phone from this rather talented pilot and am amazed to find it is slightly scratched but still fully functional. This is a little surprising as this same mobile phone has similarly been dropped three or four times in the last six months. I suspect that the bad design of the belt clip on this particular model may be a ploy to sell even more new phones.

What is really astonishing is that this technology is so resilient against such huge acceleration and deceleration. At a modest estimate, the g-force exerted on the phone when it hit the floor must have been in excess of 30g. Such a force would kill a human instantly and only ten years ago would have seen a mobile phone inoperable and smashed to pieces. Now it doesn't even make the cover flip off or the battery fall out.

Just 25 years ago I was designing and building test equipment for applications that dictated a military standard specification. One crucial test

Modern plastics and materials tend not to break like this!

Reproduced by kind permission of BT Laboratories UK

was to take equipment and drop it from a height of 1m onto a solid concrete bed, on each corner at a time, and it still had to remain fully functional.

To say the least this was a tough specification to achieve. Even the 1m-drop test inflicted a significantly huge g-force on discrete components and could tear them from their mounting. For the designers of missiles, where forces are measured in the hundreds or thousands of g, rugged operation was an even bigger headache at that time.

What has changed? The large-scale integration of components is the key. Instead of thousands of transistors, capacitors, resistors and wire leads mounted on printed circuit boards, we now have integrated circuits bonded onto substrates devoid of leads and, more importantly, almost devoid of any significant mass. The opportunity for mechanical damage has therefore been vastly reduced over the last 25 years.

In the equation of gravitational force – $F = mg$, there is nothing you can do about g, unless you leave the planet, so reducing m is the only variable at our disposal. So if you reflect on the size and weight reduction of mobile phones over the past 12 years, it is clear we have gone from around 1kg to around 0.01kg, a reduction of >100:1. And so then has the force when we drop technology.

Mobile phones, wrist watches, pocket calculators, cameras, voice recorders, MP3 players and more are now achieving a robustness and operational capability in excess of military expectation. The other major improvements have been increasingly durable plastics, able to withstand mechanical, electrical, chemical and wide range of user abuse.

In the next phase we can expect to see the components embedded in plastics and fabrics in a similar manner to the steel wire and hardcore in reinforced concrete. From thereon the trajectory is towards the production of devices that will almost literally last for ever. The single most critical components are now the I/O and battery elements, but even these are being integrated as polymer displays, batteries and touch-sensitive elements along with acoustic transducers of phenomenal performance.

Our ability to do more with less material year on year and achieve higher performance at the same time shows no sign of diminishing or slowing down. Indeed it appears to be accelerating. We already see elements of self-repair in integrated circuits, processors, displays, and storage devices, and it is becoming increasingly commonplace in all our systems.

Historically we have come from a direction of high tech and military performance migrating down to toys. Today the flow is being reversed, as our toys become increasingly leading edge and high tech, and ahead of military developments. To some extent this is due to consumer disposable income increasing while military budgets have reduced, but there are other factors too. So we see the military purchasing GPS and other IT equipment from the same sources you and I enjoy.

In the Gulf War the families were shipping GPS receivers to the troops in the desert because the mil-spec devices were unavailable at the time. And it turned out that the most reliable IT used by the military was a laser jet printer purchased from a high street store in the UK. This is a trend that is bound to accelerate with the changing nature of war, the integration of conflict into society itself, and the simultaneous availability of all technologies to all factions.

Where do we go from here? I think smart materials are the way forward, where we combine electronic processing and storage within the very fabric of everything we produce. Not so long ago a carriage clock was a big, cumbersome, expensive, relatively inaccurate and unreliable item of great value. Today we wear the time, and the wristwatch is compact, convenient, inexpensive, incredibly accurate, reliable and of little value. Mobile phones are treading the same historical path, as are PDAs, and ultimately, so will the PC and all forms of computing.

I for one would like to wear all my IT (mobile phone, camera and computer) in the same way as I wear my glasses, watch and clothing. But nobody, including me, wants to look like the back of a PC! It has to be stylish but most of all it has to be reliable, durable and extremely easy to use.

Byte 47

Naturism In Engineering

I am looking for a lot of men who have an infinite capacity to not know what can't be done.

Henry Ford

Will our manufactured life forms be a threat to us, or will they be benign?

Mother Nature engineers everything bottom up. She works on the atomic, molecular, cellular and reproductive level, with evolution taking a very slow hand in generation-by-generation change. Conversely, we start from bulk materials and work down towards the atoms and invoke massive change in a very short time, and by design we are far more disruptive than genetics. But now we also have the ability to modify the bottom-up approach, by building an atom at a time using nanotechnology and by adjusting the gene structure of biological entities and thereby the direction of evolution.

Alarmists have painted a picture of our ultimate collapse brought about by interfering with what they consider to be God's creation. I prefer a more optimistic view that can be explained as follows: if we were to take a sheet of rubber and stretch it out across the entire area of a room and scatter a handful of very heavy ball bearings onto the sheet to produce a distribution of deep depressions, we can think of these as existence areas for life. Over a period of two billion years Mother Nature has tried to create life across the entire sheet of possibilities and in the vast majority of locations she has failed. Through a slow trial-and-error evolutionary process she has created life forms that are stable and well behaved, all represented by the depressions created by the ball bearings.

Of course some of the ball bearings have been removed from our sheet as countless millions of life forms that have disappeared over the last 500 million years since the Cambrian Explosion. But we can create new opportunities by placing even more ball bearings on the sheet. Will our manufactured life forms be a threat to us, or will they be benign? I think it's an almost racing certainty that they will be both benign and short lived. This is certainly borne out by the biological weapons programmes that have had to resort to naturally occurring organisms for long-term agents, and have experienced considerable difficulties creating any long-term lethality from unnaturally created agents.

Artificially created germ warfare agents are difficult to produce and sustain and tend to be short lived. The converse is true (after billions of attempts by Mother Nature) of naturally occurring agents such as smallpox and anthrax. But even here we find that the former is a significant risk to humanity whilst the later poses almost a zero threat.

So here we are, the new boys on the block, having worked genetic miracles with natural and artificial life in a very short time, whilst Mother Nature has taken two billion years to create an astonishingly life-rich planet. I think she still has my vote in the overall scheme of things for thoroughness as she has taken time to explore all the avenues on the evolutionary tree. We on the other hand are being (of necessity) far more focused.

As far as we know, silicon life is an exception in the grand scheme of things. For reasons to do with the boundary conditions for life creation, silicon life could not have sprung from the naturally occurring environment and conditions on planet earth. Not, that is, until we arrived. That is not to say that silicon life could not have been created on some other planet, given the right conditions, but we have been the hand that created silicon life capable of evolving solutions to problems that mathematics and humans cannot solve. We have created artificial schemas where species' lifetimes are accelerated to see millions of carbon years become hours of silicon time.

This is powerful stuff that most find acceptable until they see it manifested in some anthropomorphic behaviour or form. Carbon-life-inspired software now controls elevators, power plants, telephone networks, defence and security systems; it is embodied in computer games and more. It is now

Life and intelligence by energy and speed

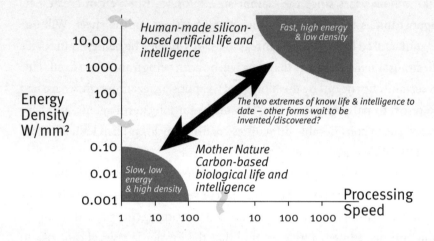

Man v machine – invention and design v evolution

By 2001, artificial life systems had re-invented many of the fundamental circuits and operations used in electronics.

The time gap between human designers and artificial life as a 'designer' is closing rapidly.

Soon we will be specifiying what we want and machines will just go away and design or evolve it for themselves!

Original invention	Year
Ladder filter	1917
Crossover filter	1925
Negative feedback amp	1927
Elliptic filter	1934
Proportional control	1939
Second order control	1942
Darlington follower	1953
Sorting network	1962
Current follower	2000
V to I converter	2000
Cubic function generator	2000
Low voltage balun	2001
Tuneable active filter	2001

in prospect of becoming the dominant mode for software creation for the majority of our support and logistics functions. It is fast, efficient, continually adaptable, and very often, the only solution available. Should we fear it? I think not! Should we be careful? Oh yes!

Silicon life will find it difficult to outclass us in the broad sense, but it is already taking us out of the loop for specific problem and control solutions. We could not control a car engine, power or manufacturing plant second by second, or even play the ultimate game of chess for example, but machines already do. But of course we still hold all the cards when it comes to creativity and emotion plus reproduction and sustainability. One reason is the storage and logic density that is currently far greater in carbon than silicon. A second is the lack of sensory perception, mobility and interconnectivity of entities. And, of course, the artificial life forms created so far have not been bottom up, but top down, or middle up. They have not started at zero to build up layer upon layer and thereby create a sustainable environment in which life can compete and be supported in the long term. But this is all a matter of complexity and connectivity of the whole, which may be solved in the next decade or two. My guess is that the turning point will be when artificial life spontaneously erupts in networks without our helping hand.

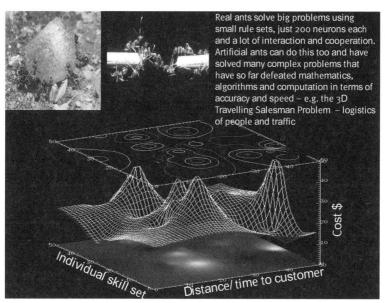

Real ants solve big problems using small rule sets, just 200 neurons each and a lot of interaction and cooperation. Artificial ants can do this too and have solved many complex problems that have so far defeated mathematics, algorithms and computation in terms of accuracy and speed – e.g. the 3D Travelling Salesman Problem – logistics of people and traffic

Reproduced by kind permission of BT Laboratories, Santa Fe Institute, and Guy Theraulaz of Centre de Recherches sur la Cognition Animale

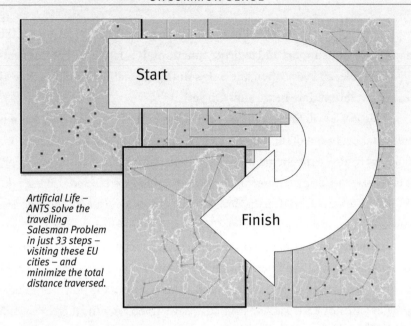

Start

Finish

Artificial Life –
ANTS solve the
travelling
Salesman Problem
in just 33 steps –
visiting these EU
cities – and
minimize the total
distance traversed.

For me, all of this will be a true turning point! I don't really fear the recreation of that scene from the movie *Terminator*, with those chilling words: 'All stealth bombers are upgraded with neural processors, becoming fully unmanned. Skynet begins to learn at a geometric rate. It becomes self-aware at 2:14 a.m. Eastern time, August 29.' And the rest, as they say, is history! What happened to Asimov's Laws of Robotics? What happened to modelling and simulation? What happened to the imagination of those working on the program? How did they get it all so badly wrong?

Asimov's laws of robotics

1 A robot may not harm a human, or, through inaction, allow a human to come to harm.
2 A robot must obey a human except where such orders would conflict with (1).
3 A robot must protect its own existence as long as this does not conflict with (1) or (2).

However, there is one slight worry I do have! Today we never invoke Asimov's Laws. From the dumbest to the smartest of robotically operated plants the machines are not programmed to protect us. And we have no equivalent laws for AI and AL. So, don't worry. I don't think anything will go wrong, go wrong, go …

Byte 48
An Invisible Revolution

*Emergent behaviour from artificial life and intelligence has pro-
duced the solutions to complex problems that defy convention.*

Ant colonies and wasp nests are good examples of simple systems exhibit-
ing complex behaviours. With minimal communication and computational
power, limited rule sets, simple software, and rudimentary sensory capability, these creatures create amazing outcomes. To date, similar bio-based
technologies have impacted telecom networks, control and logistic systems,
organizational science and crowd behaviour studies in a spectacular manner. What really appeals to me is the way in which very simple organisms
and systems are able to realize highly effective outcomes to complex and
apparently insurmountable problems.

Standing on the shoulders of Mother Nature and picking her brains
has given us an incredible short cut to success and solutions. In many respects it has also given us a precursor to some of the recently emerging
behaviours in our own society.

2000/01 saw a number of spectacular events across Europe that exhib-
ited simple organic behaviour within human networks that epitomized the
advantage of biological evolution and self-organization over hierarchy and
centralized control. A principle cause was rapidly rising petroleum prices
through excessive taxation. First was a spontaneous revolt in France, with
the blocking of roads and ports by farmers, truck and cab drivers. This was
not a unionized or centrally organized operation. There was no identifiable
leader. It was a distributed reaction using mobile phone and email to great
effect.

File   Ants   Display   Help   Tue 11 19 36

This ant colony lives in my laptop and achieves complex behaviour patterns and problem solving using very simple rules.

Rules of ant life

✳ If you find food
    ⇒ take it home marking a trail.

✳ If you cross a trail and you have no food
    ⇒ follow the trail to the food.

✳ If you return home with food
    ⇒ put it down and return up the trail.

✳ Otherwise
    ⇒ wander at random looking for food.

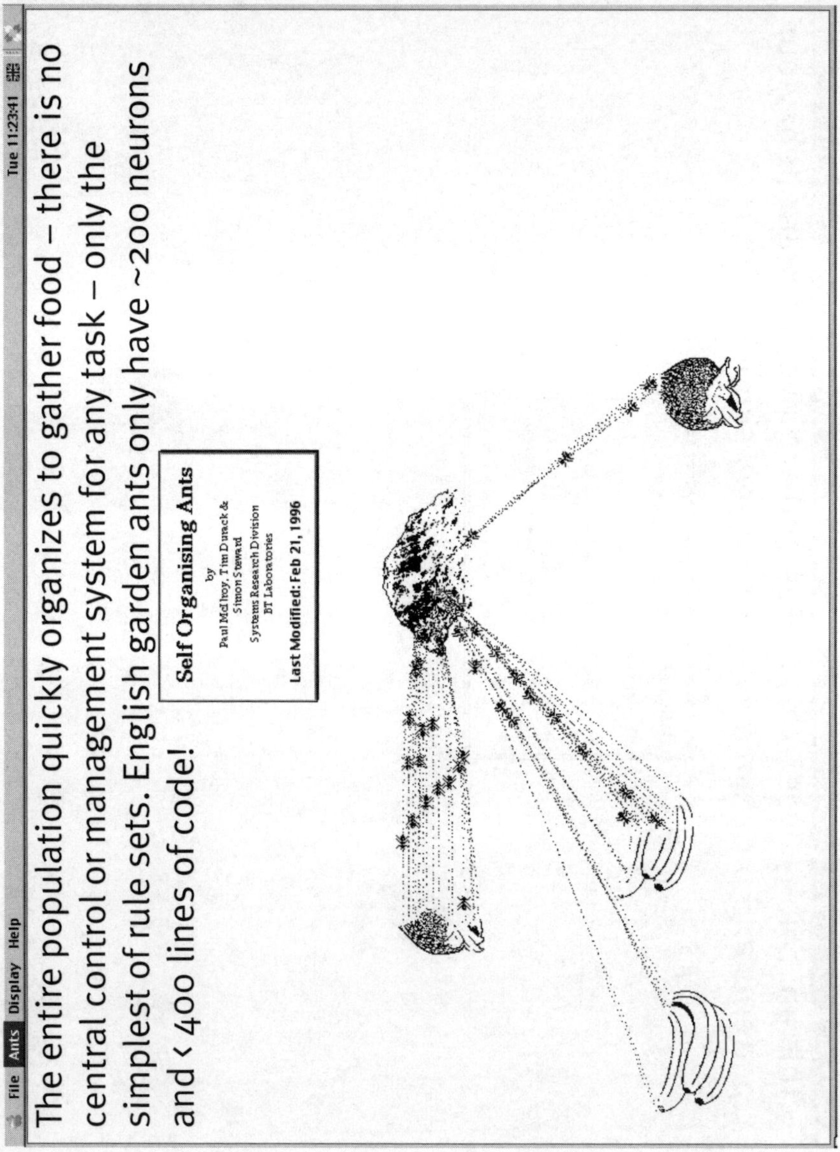

File Ants Display Help
Tue 11:23:41

The entire population quickly organizes to gather food – there is no central control or management system for any task – only the simplest of rule sets. English garden ants only have ~200 neurons and < 400 lines of code!

Self Organising Ants

by
Paul McIlroy, Tim Dunnck &
Simon Steward
Systems Research Division
BT Laboratories

Last Modified: Feb 21, 1996

Other European nations joined the rebellion rapidly. Governments didn't see it coming. Their public radar system was ineffective and their shields were down. By the time heads of state appeared on TV to appeal for calm the protestors were in distributed control and far better informed and organized than government. And as soon as a government spokesman made accusations of intimidation and violence to bolster the position of the police and military, a TV reporter would be on screen with denial interviews involving the people on the ground. Those who were supposedly being defended and protected by government were publicly rejecting that proposition as unnecessary since the claimed intimidation had never occurred. What a coup – Government 0 – Rebellion 1.

Just picture it: information arrives at some regional government office to be filtered and distorted as it passes from one layer to another. Advisors are consulted and a committee formed to decide the best course of action. Strategists, PR people, and spin doctors apply their wisdom, the appropriate politician gives it a tweak, and all is set for presenting to the electorate by the head of state. In the meantime, the protestors have disseminated the latest developments across the country and moved on to the next phase. Their silent and invisible electronic network is operating in a distributed mode thousands of times faster than that of the paper and word-of-mouth world of the government.

The final curtain was superbly timed. A country was close to collapse and a state of emergency was being declared. As the military were about to remove the blockages because food and energy supplies were obviously threatened, the protesters at the blockades spontaneously disappeared and even more public support was gained. In such a situation, zero hierarchy and speed of communication are clear winners. This was guerrilla warfare without casualties, other than the loss of face by government. In such a game it is speed and direction of decision that win the day against depth of thought and old thinking.

A parallel situation preceded the EU fuel rebellion with the very tragic loss of the Russian nuclear submarine Kursk on 12 August 2000. This turned out to be an awful example of 'not understanding' by a state. Here was an old military and party machine accustomed to controlling the media and flow of information for decades. Delays, untruths, attempts at a cover up, accusations of interference from outside forces, a possible collision with a another vessel, the denial of clearly registered explosions, were all used to hide the truth. Offers of help by other nations were rejected as unnecessary, and false hopes were created by stories of communication with the crew of the stricken sub. Why? To save face and avert blame?

The communications channels of the planet were ahead of the military and political machine by days. The bits just outpaced the atoms and the distributed intelligence of the Internet went far beyond the government players. Public anger quickly mounted and political credibility was lost at a rapidly accelerating rate. Reports from the outside world of an explosion at 11:29hrs of 1.5 on the Richter scale (corresponding to 100kg of high explosives), followed by another at 11.31 of magnitude 3.5 immediately negated all the official versions of the incident.

It is hard to say how many similar situations have occurred in the past, but no doubt a lot has gone unreported or misrepresented. It will be increasingly difficult for governments to do so in the future as technology opens more communication channels and information freedom. The old controlist managers and regimes may have to retire before we see a complete change, but I suspect that day may be brought ever closer if they are unable to respond to the changes being enacted by societies through technology. Most recently the SARS outbreak in China prompted an attempt by government ministers and officials to cover up and downplay the scale of the problem, and led to the sacking of those responsible. It also became clear that the containment operation was significantly hampered and delayed by the attempted cover up – and people died as a result. Global communication in all its forms will increasingly preclude such actions in the future and, moreover, become essential in preventing future pandemics, should they arise.

If you are going to tell lies or deal in half-truths you have to be brilliant – you need such an incredible memory and global control – you have to be in a position, and have the technology, to control the source and flow of information over all forms of network. The sequence of events and timing also has to be perfect. All of this was possible in the past, but not any more!

Byte 49
The Lull Before – Smarter Machines?

By 2020 I expect all our devices to be making intelligent decisions about steering messages across a room or through a building, instead of the dumb routings of today.

Every now and again the IT industry seems to hit a lull where there seems to be very little happening. I think we're in such a lull right now. Many see our present range of devices as being the future, with an ideal form factor and performance that will see us through the coming decade. I don't agree. I think what we have is rapidly becoming boring. For sure it is magical in its performance and abilities, but there have been no fundamental changes for the last five years. Yes, our devices have become smaller and displays have got bigger, and interfaces have become a little friendlier, but the reality is that the PC, PDA, mobile phone and laptop are pretty much the same as those we had five years ago. The question is – will this continue, and for how long?

In the past year I have seen chip technologies that will reduce the power consumption ~10-fold and new system design techniques that will give further reductions by a factor ~6×. There are also new antenna technologies that are ~4× more efficient, displays that require no back lighting and data storage devices that are ~100× more dense than today. Then there are fuel cells with ~20× the energy density, and interfaces that are almost human. I think we should think of technology progress and change in several dimensions. We can only guess at the benefits devices that are $10 \times 6 \times 4 \times 20 \times 100 = 480,000\times$ more powerful, or 100× smaller than today, for the same equivalent functionality.

The practicality of really small devices may of course be defeated, in some sense, by the size of our fingers, the wavelength of sound and the

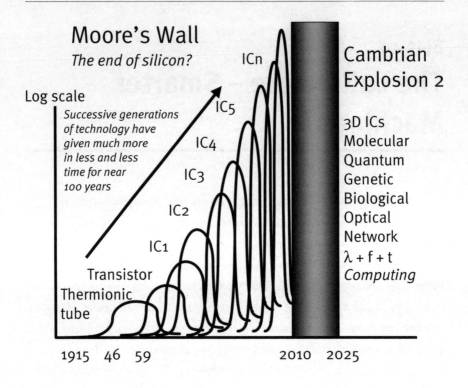

Moore's Wall
The end of silicon?

ICn

Cambrian
Explosion 2

Log scale

*Successive generations
of technology have
given much more
in less and less
time for near
100 years*

IC5

IC4

IC3

IC2

IC1

Transistor

Thermionic
tube

3D ICs
Molecular
Quantum
Genetic
Biological
Optical
Network
λ + f + t
Computing

1915   46   59   2010   2025

distance between ear and mouth, but there is much more to come. Devices capable of storing every movie and music track ever recorded are not beyond the realms of physical possibility and will ultimately arrive.

If we factor in the long-term impact of exponential increases in chip performance and bit density, we are looking at more than one billion times over the next 30 years. At some point we will hit the physical limits currently designated as Moore's Wall. Here our semi-conductor technologies come to the end of the road as we approach the physical limits dictated by the size of individual atoms and their subatomic components. Our best guess is that Moore's Wall will occur sometime around 2020. But, even by 2006, Intel are predicting that their microprocessors will be clocking at 10GHz – 3 × faster than today. We can anticipate far greater rates by 2020 and memory capacities measured in PetaBytes (*1PByte = 1000TByte = 1,000,000GByte = 1,000,000,000MByte = approximately one thousand million paperback novels' worth!*). There may also come a time when the difference between RAM and hard drive will have been eliminated as irrelevant.

Beyond 2020 and Moore's Wall, we see a lot of uncertainty, but an even bigger range of options than today. There will be far more technology riches than we have enjoyed to date since the invention of the thermionic tube by DeForest in 1915. I think it is reasonable to assume devices at least one hundred billion times more powerful than today. What would such devices bring us? I think they will be machines of great intelligence, with location and state awareness, cognition and contextualization, and with the ability to continuously and automatically configure to a dynamic world. They will anticipate our needs and operate to our specific and individual benefit, and hopefully they will take away the tyranny of the GUI.

Today I travel the planet reconfiguring my mobile phone and laptop for different operating bands, carriers and regimes. Generally, none of the functions are fully automatic and switching between hotel, home, and company LAN, wireless LAN, dial-up modem and other modes is a pain. As I visit companies, universities and individuals, nothing is easy. If only it was all automated and I could just switch on and go. I really do not need to get involved in selecting the network and setting up the devices to establish communication. If all my files and support systems could be automatically updated as I travel, how much more efficient I would be.

By 2020 I expect all our devices to be making intelligent decisions about steering messages across a room or through a building, instead of the dumb routings of today. I expect location-based activities and state to be subsumed into my devices so that they can make sensible decisions about my travel, work and communication. I need far less overload and far more effectiveness that only intelligent machines can give me. I need technology to augment my existence, to detect when I am tired, hungry or busy, so that I can be automatically steered towards the right activities and decisions.

At a modest estimate my work output has been increasing tenfold every decade for the past 40 years and it has now started to stall. The principle reason is that the human aspects of technology are not advancing fast enough. Without intelligent machines I cannot increase my augmented intelligence and output.

Will intelligent machines sell? Look at the sales of intelligent vacuum cleaners, lawn mowers and robotic pets for the home. People empathize with animals and anything remotely intelligent, even if it is technology. Adding personality and personalization to all the coming technologies will be essential if we are to maintain, let alone increase, our individual progress. A lot of workplace stress can be traced back to rising management expectation that goes unsupported by adequate or sufficient system support. The really good news is: if we don't get to it and engineer a fix, then our machines will evolve into that role even without our help – it will just take a little longer!

Byte 50
Sleep?

Perhaps our role on this planet is no longer to worship the gods, but to build them so we may understand cause and effect and manage our societies and futures?

By the time you have got to these words I hope you have read a sufficient number of the preceding Bytes to concur with me when I say that writing a book about technology and its implications is not like writing about history, cooking or romance. Technology is inconvenient; it has neither beginning, nor end, nor middle, nor conclusion; it is never right or wrong, good or evil, passive or inconsequential; and it is never static. Technology never sleeps, never stops, never concludes, but evolves with us as a part of our wider human story. We are now a part of our own technology and vice versa. Without it we would be nothing, and for some time to come the converse will also be true. Everything we know, understand and achieve is by the hand of technology, and by this hand we have yet to discover more than any of us can imagine.

If you are one of those people who start at the back of book, dive into the middle, and then go to the beginning, or just randomly sample pages before reading the whole in some kind of order, or perhaps not at all, I can only encourage you to dive into the text somewhere – *several times*. Read, look at the pictures and diagrams, think, and form your own views. After 46 years of being steeped in science, technology and engineering, I have already done so! And it is no accident that a part of my time and energy has been, and continues to be, devoted to communicating the implications of what we have done, are doing, and are about to do.

The overall and complete picture of science and technology, the crea-tion of sustainable futures, benefiting and advancing humankind, the well-being of other species and the planet, is well beyond any book, and certainly well beyond the human mind. The carbon deposits on this white backdrop can never convey what we have done, and what we are about. This limited medium and this limited author can only offer a few samples, mere teasers, of technologies and issues that are, or will become, increasingly important and critical to all of us as we advance into this 21st century.

At best we can describe our journey in abstractions that gloss over any detail or problems, and at worst we can drill down to the minutiae and completely miss all the relationships and the big picture. I have chosen a middle(ish) path – to take samples along our increasingly broad timeline of invention and innovation – charting some of the immediate (or near immediate) implications for individuals and society. Some may think the content to be tongue in cheek – but it isn't. Some may think it controversial, radical, unlikely, or even scary – maybe!

The reality is – this is just a sample, a very small sample, of an exponentially growing landscape (see Byte 08) of development that is accelerating away from our ancient past and ways of thinking. The question is: do we want to be spectators or players, victims or contributors? As the subject is beyond a single book, and having no idea if I will ever write another in this series of Bytes, I can only direct you to my home page, (www.cochrane.org.uk) where you will find over 1000 articles, papers, writings, movie and sound files, plus links to hundreds of other very interesting sites. These may further help you, as they help many others, to embrace more fully what is happening.

The biggest danger to our species, and others, is that we give up trying to understand, we stop searching for the truth, and we rail back our progress. We did just that once before, and those dark ages, with those dark minds, benefited no one. The potential of science and technology as a force for good and the creation of a positive future for all has never been so great. BUT, we all have to make an effort to understand, subsume the new, and change the way we manage, operate and govern.

So this is not shut down or switch off, but sleep ...

Every animal leaves traces of what they were; man alone leaves traces of what he created.

Jacob Bronowski

Index

ERAU-PRESCOTT LIBRARY

WITHDRAWN